Olive Juice

...and other thoughts on love, heartbreak and moving forward.

eric champnella

diag productions

OLIVE JUICE

. . . and other thoughts on love, heartbreak and moving forward

by Eric Champnella

Published by:
Diag Productions
11271 Ventura Blvd., P.O. Box #132
Studio City, California 91604

Email: olivejuice@olivejuicebook.com

cover design by Cheryl Gaskill
cover art direction by Betty Halpern

First Printing 2000

Printed in the United States of America

Publisher's Cataloging-in-Publication
(Provided by Quality Books, Inc.)

Champnella, Eric
Olive juice : -- and other thoughts on love, heartbreak, and moving forward / Eric Champnella. -- 1st ed.
p.cm.
LCCN: 00-190366
ISBN: 0-9679755-5-7

1. Separation (Psychology) 2. Interpersonal relations. 3. Couples. 4. Man-woman relationships. I. Title.

HQ801.A3C53 2000 306.73
QBI00-346

CONTENTS

OLIVE JUICE

PREFACE

I must admit that writing this "preface" part, these few paragraphs, was the most daunting task of writing this "book" you are about to read. It's taken me more time and thought and energy and re-writing of this simple little opening than any 20 pages to follow. This part right here. This looking-back-in-hindsight preface portion that most people will probably skip over anyway, as I often do with any pages in a book numbered with roman numerals and not good ol' "1, 2, 3, 4...". That's because it seems like the "book" that follows was written long ago. During a different time. By a different me.

It's a strange feeling, gazing back on words that literally burst forth with such emotion I was sometimes surprised they came from me, yet whose reading now leaves me almost bewildered at their source. Not that the source was disingenuous, just now tucked deep inside; the only difference nothing more than an outlook edited by time. Kind of like rummaging through an old drawer and stumbling across a yellowed scrap of paper containing an 8th grade love letter written oh-so-many years ago with the uncompromising hopefulness of a schoolboy's passion, only to have those very same words on that aging paper bring forth a small introspective smile today. For the boy that was and the man he has become. And so I look at these words you are about to read almost like a stranger secretly flipping through the pages of another's diary. Unable to turn away.

This didn't start out as a book. It started out simply as my journal (hence the reason I put the word "book" in quotes above). I initially wrote the following pages just for myself. To get me through a tough time after the sudden end of a long-term relationship. So while some may call this a self-help book, for me it is, and was, a self-ish-help book. Just a guy searching in pen to paper for answers. And while I don't know if that search is complete (or if it ever is), I know this "book", and its purpose in my life, are.

And so, I pass it on to you.

I would like to thank numerous friends (many mentioned on the pages to follow) for this book making its long and winding path into your hands. Up until a short time ago, these pages were nothing more than a pals-only manuscript, passed along to those friends who were going through a similarly tough time or to those who knew someone who was. If not for their heartfelt responses and frequent urgings, I'm pretty sure the following pages would ultimately have been banished to a 200,000k space in the farthest reaches of my computer's hard drive; to be printed out and passed along to trusted confidants as the need or request arose.

It is also due to these same friends that the above-mentioned 200,000k file didn't end up in your hands at about 20k. That's because the more I read it, consequently looking back on events and heartache long since tempered by time and perspective, I kept editing it and cutting it and trimming it until I think instead of a book, it was on it's way to becoming an article. Because time had taken its course. Healing. Soothing. Fixing. And some of the chapters written by yesterday's me didn't evoke the same response from today's. Thus, I continued to chop and whittle away. Until many a friend pointed out that the reason it didn't "sound the same" was because I've moved on. Past the stage that drove me to write the words that follow. But for many others they said, unwittingly (and unwantingly) stuck right where I was a few years back, these same words I now questioned would resonate with them, eliciting the very feelings that were now beginning to fade for me. And that was, and is, the whole point of this "book."

So, here are the passages that I kept (and the others that my trusted friends convinced me to put back). They are a collection of my journal entries, poems, musings and other thoughts as I was writing this in "book" form. There is no structure. There is no beginning, middle and end per se for in life, I have learned, one never really knows at the time when the end of one chapter is coming to a close and the beginning of a totally new book is about to begin. Nope. You'll only know after the fact.

Also keep in mind that the following is going to contain paradoxes and contradictions galore. Why? Because that's just how life is. It doesn't make sense. So when you read something on one page that seems to be totally at odds with what you just finished reading on the previous page - sorry. I didn't plan it that way. It's just how life ends up sometimes. Or should I say, all too often.

I must also tell you I'm not a psychologist, psychiatrist, minister, therapist, counselor, sociologist, doctor or any other such "trained" expert in the study or dealings of human relationships. Rather, I am just like you. I'm just another human being like you who went through some of the same things that drove you to pick up this book in the first place. In short, I'm the teacher, the banker, the lawyer, the clerk, the janitor, the homemaker and even the therapist, counselor, and others with the one thing we all have in common - Life.

If you're looking for "expert" opinion backed up by years of research and office training, put this book down and grab another. These are just my thoughts, opinions and own personal discoveries. I shared them out of a need and a hope -

a need to understand for myself and a hope to shed some light for others. I don't claim anything more. Like many of you reading this, my only official "study" of psychology came from the required classes I took in college. My "training" coming from the one school we all graduated from - the proverbial School of Hard Knocks.

So hopefully you didn't pick this book up in the psychology section of the bookstore. Nor the self-help aisle. No, hopefully you found it in a tiny, little, new heading...Life.

Finally, I hope I'm not being too pretentious thinking any thoughts or experiences I've had can be of any value to anyone else. I can only wish that to be the case. If you read this and just enjoy it for the read, that's fine. But if you read it and get just one thing out of it, that's even better. I'll be smiling somewhere.

Eric Champnella

PREFACE II:

The Y Chromosome Version

A side note to any guys currently perusing these pages in the store aisle while constantly looking over their shoulder to make sure no one sees them reading THIS book: I know. I understand. Believe me. After I finished the friend's-draft way back when, I didn't give a copy to most of my buddies for the longest time. And then, even after showing them and getting the same positive feedback, I was still a tad skeptical as to whether or not fellow men would admit to buying this book (probably myself included if I hadn't written it). That's because we're coached since birth that we're not supposed to like or understand books like this (and we sure as hell aren't supposed to write them). As men, we're supposed to play with pain not show it. Therefore, on the following page, I have included an alternate, tear-out cover. Think of it as the Y Chromosome Version. The one you can leave laying around the office. So, if you intend to purchase this yet don't exactly want the rest of the world to know you're buying it, simply rip out the following page and place it over the regular cover before you approach the cashier.

Glad I could help,

Eric

GREATEST
SPORTS
MOMENTS
OF ALL TIME
By Joe Sport

HERE GOES...

For some reason I have been driven to start writing my journal entries in "this" form. I don't know what "this" is or where it's heading, but I just kind of feel the need to go with it and start writing.

You see, I've recently been faced with one of the most painful things that has ever happened to me and while it has truly broken my heart, the event has energized my thought process. I've been doing a lot of thinking lately. And believe it or not, I may actually have learned a few things. I suppose that's up to you to decide. I guess I just wanted to see if I could do some good. If my pain hopefully wasn't all for naught. For, if my words and experiences can help even one person, can add just a little comfort somewhere or, in the best of all possible cases, if I could actually prevent someone from traveling down this path, then I guess in some ways it might have actually been for a reason.

Maybe this is about moving forward. About

letting go of the unchangeable past, not worrying about the unpredictable future and just living in the some-semblance-of-control here and now. The present.

It's about searching for answers. Answers for some questions I don't even know to ask yet. It's a quest. It's a trip. It's a journey. It's about life.

LEARNING EXPERIENCES

The most painful lessons any of us will ever go through are life's so called "learning experiences." Unfortunately, I've heard the phrase just a little too often lately. That's a signal. If people are telling you, on a regular basis, that what you're going through is a so-called "learning experience," chances are, your life isn't exactly going as planned right at this particular moment. You're going through a tough time - a.k.a. a "learning experience."

If you doubt me, next time you're in the midst of a crisis, count how many times your friends and family use the term. Put it this way, if you got a dime for every time the phrase was used, your problems probably would be lessened or at least eased merely by the financial windfall.

I still haven't figured out why learning experiences always have to be bad things. I've yet to overhear someone say, "You're not going to believe it! I opened my door last night and Miss America was standing on my porch holding a six-pack and the winning Lotto ticket. Boy, what a learning experience that was for me!"

Nope. Never heard that. Not once. Learning experiences are the events that shape your soul. Test your mettle. And if these learning experiences are indeed life's toughest pop quizzes, then love has got to be the Ph.D. dissertation of the lot. And the end of love is the unfortunate graduation ceremony.

In case you hadn't guessed, I have just gone through - correction, am going through - one of these learning experiences. I don't know if my soul is being shaped but I do know one thing for sure - my heart was broken. It's been quite a learning experience. I've learned that love isn't just a word or part of a convenient phrase. Love is a gift. Love is alive. Love is magic. I knew that before. And that was my mistake. I knew it. Like a scientist knows an equation. Like an athlete knows a move. My problem was I didn't live it.

No, wait, that isn't absolutely correct either. I lived and felt it, but I didn't treat love with the respect it deserved. Oh sure, I kept Hallmark in business for a few years. F.T.D. was a big beneficiary of mine. MCI stock rose during the course of my relationship. No, what I'm trying to point out is I didn't realize just how precious a "thing" love was. Did I take it for granted? Yes, of course, to some degree. But it is different than that, too. My mistake was out of ignorance. I didn't understand just how incredible and fleeting love is. I didn't know that love is what makes all things possible. I didn't have any idea that nothing can replace love.

Now don't for a minute think I thought buying an occasional card or sending flowers was love. Wrong. I do - nor did - not. That's the point. I did those things, knew they weren't love, still was in love and yet, somehow, apparently didn't know what the hell love was. Confused? Me, too. And yet I'm ten times clearer on this subject now than I ever used to be. See, there's the answer. If you think you know what love is, are currently living a dictionary or Hallmark-defined definition of love, chances are that isn't it. Capiche? There is no answer to "What is love?" It just is. It's when you pass from the point of "knowing" what love is and "knowing" you're in it to just being. That's it. Love is. Period. Once you can sum up your "love" in one sentence like a book synopsis, look out. There's trouble in paradise.

OLIVE JUICE

THAT ANNOYING GRAIN OF HOPE

Long after you know it's over, there is still something that must be wrestled with. It is The Irrational Thought. The Unjustified Maybe. The Never Ending Possibility. It is what I call "That Annoying Grain of Hope."

Now, "That Annoying Grain of Hope" doesn't come right after your world blows up and there is still uncertainty as to whether or not what happened is indeed what happened. Nope. It's well past that shell-shocked stage. "That Annoying Grain of Hope" rears its ugly head long after the phone has stopped ringing. Beyond the point of sent and received letters. Further down the road when that single blinking red flash on your answering machine actually *is* who you said it probably was to your roommate (when deep in your heart you secretly hoped...).

"That Annoying Grain of Hope" usually shows up when your friends are saying to each other, "Gee, (YOUR NAME HERE) sure is dealing with that well." When asked, you tell everyone that yes, it is still hard, but you're moving forward and not looking back.

And you even may believe that when you say it.

However, I think "That Annoying Grain of Hope" is just pain masked; hurt that everybody (read "everybody" here to mean those who have never been through something like this) thinks you should be past. Pain that is still there so it has to surface somehow. And it appears in perhaps the cruelest way of all - disguised as hope. Hope that even the inner voice inside us all says is not justified. Not rational. Yet we so want to believe.

This perverted distortion of Hope makes its appearance when the pain has shifted from the it-hurts-every-minute-of-every-waking-day to something deeper. A sense of unaccepted finality.

Your head knows (and it's true) that it's over but your heart is fighting the losing battle of its life. I think that's because in order to understand all this and to be able to see it, one's heart must be whole. In one's heart lies the ability to see reason. Not the mind. And once the heart is broken...

"That Annoying Grain of Hope" is merely unaccepted finality. And because we feel it as Hope, this is the time when we are most vulnerable to doing stupid things: The phone call we make out of the blue, the letter that will correct all, the unannounced visit because we feel a last ditch sense of omnipotence regarding our situation. Some emotional Last Stand that is sure to work.

Don't be fooled.

One positive about doing one of the above-mentioned "stupid things" is they usually end up killing that hope and turning it back into the unaccepted finality it really is. When the call is short and cold. When the letter goes unanswered. When the unannounced visit reveals an unknown third party.

Did I mention that when I said "Last Stand" I was thinking of Custer?

OLIVE JUICE

PIECE OF MY HEART...?

I'll never love anyone the same or as much again. There will never be this intensity. Never this level of emotional depth. Never the totality of feelings. Etc., etc., etc.

Sound familiar?

When this all broke, I told my friend Jessica that I felt sorry for the girl that I ultimately ended up with because my ex would always have a piece of my heart. A small part of me that no one could ever have. There would be this little space, way down deep, that I would never be able to give to another because she would always have it. Forever. It was just a fact of life and there was nothing I could do about it. It wasn't that I would want to "keep" a piece of my heart away from my future whoever, rather it was out of my control. Like when a vase shatters, as hard as you may try, you simply cannot find each and every one of the little shards to put the sucker back together in its pre-shattered form. It can't be done. Some little piece will inevitably end up missing. And so I told my friend my theory.

But my friend had her own theory. Jessica, who was divorced, had just recently started seeing someone seriously again for the first time since. She was truly in love and as happy as I'd ever seen her. And she told me something that really stayed with me. She said that my theory was just the pain speaking and I was wrong; that when I met the person I would spend the rest of my life with, when I met "The One," my theory would come crashing apart just like my previously-mentioned vase. She believed, from experience, I would be able to give away my entire heart again because at that point, K. would no longer have a piece of my heart. Not an ounce. Not the smallest shred or morsel. Nope, my heart, the whole kit'n'caboodle, would belong to someone else...and all K. would have would be a small piece of my memory.

When Jessica first told me this, I thought it sounded great. Had kind of a nice hopeless romantic ring to it. Even made a nice counterpoint theory to my own. But I felt, in actuality, when tested, when her hypothesis came under the rigors of life, she was wrong.

Well, I stand corrected. Now that some time has passed I have to admit she was right. Wow. I guess the heart isn't like a vase after all. Because it's not a "thing" that can be broken in the permanent sense. The heart is a feeling. The heart is hope. The heart is your dreams. And while feelings can definitely be hurt, while hope can be diminished, while dreams can be dashed, these things can never be "broken" for good. They can't be taken away forever. Because somewhere down the road, whether we want to or not, our heart will start the process of life up all over again. With or without our consent. And no matter how far down we were, how impossible it once seemed, the heart will heal itself. Just when we thought "never" was an option, lo and behold, the heart we'd once thought unusable will start to feel again. The heart that once seemed drained of all things precious will hope again. The heart that once felt forever "broken" will dare to dream again.

The heart is not a vase. It's a home. The home of life. So I sit here with a small smile. I've been doing a lot of cleaning in my "home." It's been a lot of work at times but I'm getting it back in shape. I'm clearing out the past for the other heart that will someday come into my home. A home once again filled with feeling, with hopes, with dreams. They may not all come true or turn out as planned but that's not the point. They are here again. In the home of my heart. So I take the last box of my past, a past that I thought would sit forever in this home, and move it up to the attic of my memory.

OLIVE JUICE

ON FALLING STARS, FRIENDS AND LISTENING

Eric,

You won't be sad forever. Remember, at some point, two stars fell from the sky at the same time and you don't know when they're going to both hit the ground.

Marcie

My friend Marcie secretly slipped that little note into my coat pocket one night after I had been spilling my guts to her as she patiently listened. It was one of those nights in the beginning when the pain seemed permanent. When hope was still a dirty word. When "someone else out there" sounded like a Hollywood fantasy.

Yet as my friend listened to me that night, (and I mean really listened, not judged or critiqued, or chastised or hurried me up like she had somewhere else to be, but just listened) I felt, even way back then, that it was going to be ok. That just maybe I would get through the hardest of hard times at hand. And all my friend had to do was listen.

It's funny, but so many times we hear about the power of the spoken word and how the pen is mightier than the sword but I'd like to cast a vote for the ear. For just being there to listen. The power of the listener. For haven't we all felt comforted in those trying moments by someone just lending a sympathetic ear? No words need to be said. No opinions voiced. Just the quiet understanding of a friend during a time of need.

One good thing about a crisis, you really find out who your friends are. And you know what? They may not be the people you initially thought they were. You'll find out very quickly that there's a big difference between a "friend" who's always there to "hang" when it's "fun" and a friend who's there to comfort when it's not.

And what really touches the heart is when you discover the true mettle behind someone you didn't initially know that well. When an acquaintance turns into a friend for life. You always hear about these life crises being for a reason, well just maybe these newly "discovered" friends are that reason. The oft-mentioned diamonds in the (very, very deep) rough.

To finish the story I started above, I didn't find Marcie's note until I got home that night. But when I did, it gave me chills.

I still have that note. I'll keep it forever.

Sometimes, when I'm feeling lonely or down, I reach into my drawer and pull it out. When I do, I usually can't help but read it more than once. It's just not something that you can simply glance at quickly and toss back into the drawer. So I read it two or three times. And whenever I do that, somehow I don't feel as lonely anymore. I don't feel quite as blue. Most of the time a small smile even sneaks across my face. All because of two stars falling. Because someone cared enough to listen.

OLIVE JUICE

JFK, THE SPACE SHUTTLE AND THE PERSIAN GULF WAR

THE CRISIS as it has now come to be known (And believe me, it is *the* crisis. Not a crisis. Not some crisis. No, *THE* crisis) has a special spot in my memory usually reserved only for history-altering events and great catastrophes. Like the assassination of President John F. Kennedy for my parents' generation or the explosion of the space shuttle Challenger and the start of the Persian Gulf War for mine, I can tell you exactly where I was and what was happening all around me when this personal history-altering, great catastrophe of mine took place.

Please know it has nothing to do with dwelling on the issue. It's not by choice. It's just there. Like my own private Zapruder film of getting dumped. Only there is no road sign to obscure any important moments nor any second gunman hiding in the grassy knoll (There was however, as I have now learned through recently declassified sources - i.e. her friends and family -

a "someone else" waiting to take my place. Thus confirming the once-controversial Second Boyfriend Theory.)

I think if one were to examine the body, one would find that the shots were fired from the rear because, quite frankly, I did not see this coming at all. And I think one more review of the now-infamous film will confirm my suspicions.

WARNING: The following contains graphic, sometimes horrifying depictions of a relationship gone askew. Please use viewer discretion if young children or those who find themselves in a seemingly blissful situation are present.

Ok, just a second here while I dim the lights. Let me just thread this last bit of the film and - there!

Rolling...

Ah, it's a beautiful day. Somewhere around the six and a half year mark of the relationship. A recent vacation has confirmed that this is to finally be the year of the big engagement. We've waited for both of us to finish school. Put things on hold so both of us could get our difficult career choices jumpstarted. But now, finally, the time is as right as it will ever be in dealing with matters of love. Also, unknown to the future Mrs., a substantial amount of money has been socked away for just the right ring. The perfect topper for the big event about to come.

And it was mutual. A phone call two days before from my Soon-To-Be ended with her saying, "I can't wait until we get married."

Ah, love...

And if you glance to the left side of the screen ladies and gentlemen, here it comes. The motorcade of my life rounding the corner heading toward the center of Happily Ever After Plaza.

Joyous applause can be heard from those lining the motorcade route:

"You two make such a wonderful couple."

"It's really no surprise to any of us. We knew it from the moment you guys started dating."

"My family loves you. How many children do you want to have?"

"She's such a sweet girl, son. I see nothing but the best for you both."

Suddenly, two, possibly three shots ring out. Literally.

Ring. Ring. Ri...

"Hello"

(LONG PAUSE) "Uhhh...Hi, Eric."

"Hi. How come you didn't call last night? Where were you?"

An eerie silence befalls the Plaza area. The motorcade begins to weave slightly with that Pit-of-the-Stomach fear when suddenly the last and final shot is fired. The one all the experts agree to be the fatal shot. The Magic Bullet.

Crack!

"Listen Eric...I've met someone else. But that has nothing to do with it. I'm breaking up because we don't want the same things anymore."

Nooooooo!!!!

And that's when things became very fuzzy.

Actually if we replay the critical last moments of the tape frame by frame, I think you can actually see a piece of my heart go flying off the back of the limousine on "I'm breaking up..." That's when unknown friends and family attempted to climb on the trunk and save it as I clutched my chest. But to no avail. It was too late. Attempts at revival proved to be futile.

As you can clearly see on the tape, that's when all hell broke loose in Happily Ever After Plaza.

Don't want the same things anymore!?!? No kidding! I don't want her sleeping with the new guy!

Hold on a second, let me turn this damn thing off and flip the lights back on.

Click.

Wow. Still gory to see again. Even after all this time has passed.

I've played and replayed the events leading up to that point over in my mind a thousand times. In fact, every couple of months, a new theory comes up. Sometimes these new theories are my own (when she said she couldn't wait until we got married, I guess my mistake was assuming I was the other half of that "we"). Other times these theories are generated by newly discovered witnesses ("A friend of her friend's friend heard..."). A virtual cottage industry of possibilities. Yet nothing, no re-examination of the events, ever seems to lead to any clear-cut answers. Only more questions.

So while the "case" may never truly be solved from this end - the dumpee end - it has been labeled "Case Closed." It doesn't really matter anymore. Besides, even the "truth" - if there is such a thing to both parties in this type of situation - would probably only lead to additional Theories. So, no more.

And yet, every now and then, I just can't help taking one last peek:

And here comes the motorcade...

Hold on! Stop the tape! I think I see something! A clue I missed!

I wonder if I should call the *Enquirer*?

OLIVE JUICE

THE PROCESS

As I write this now in "book" form, I keep referring back to my journal I kept during that period. Since time is starting to cloud my emotions and memories, I need those words of pages and days past to keep my muse for these pages and days present going.

It's kind of a strange and weird feeling to keep looking over that journal. While doing it serves a purpose for me (and you, the reader) from a writing standpoint, I have to admit it's kind of tough on an emotional level. Tends to pick at healing wounds. It feels like I'm returning over and over again to the scene of some near-fatal car wreck I survived for one last look. Like emotional rubber necking. "God, what a horrible accident...let's go get another look."

But by the same token, if I had never gone through everything, I would have never written this book. Not a chance. This isn't something I could've penned by merely talking to others who've had similar experiences. Nope. I had to run the gauntlet myself to find the words. The meaning. The truth. Strange thing is, I might never know if it was for any good. Served any purpose. Helped one person. That's because, first of all, I'm writing this right now on my computer in the bedroom of my little apartment in Southern California. It's early January. No book publisher awaits. No promises were made. No one (except for my mom) even knows I'm writing "A BOOK."

Actually, I should be asleep. It's late at night. I should be in bed getting rested for my job tomorrow. The guaranteed job. The one that has paid my rent on a regular basis.

Yet I am driven to write these words. Finish these thoughts. Compose these sentences for...what? For whom? I don't know yet, but I hope. Hope that somehow, someway, this gets to somebody, somewhere who is touched by it. Who feels a little less troubled. A little less lost. A little more hope.

But you know, it has already helped one person. Made one soul feel a little better in the above aspects. That person is me. Am I staying up nights just writing this for me? Who knows at this point, but it feels pretty good writing it, so I can only hope that it will feel as good to read for someone else.

Someday.

So with that hope "out there," I continue to look back. Back over often painful notes. Often painful memories. I look back so that I can share with you and share with myself. Share the process of healing.

And as I re-read those journal pages, I'm also struck by something else: How at some of my lowest points came some of the very words that I am most proud of and most surprised by. The very things I am trying to capture on these pages you now read. It's amazing to me now because, on a conscious level, writing in that journal just seemed like an exercise in futility. Something to do until night fell and I could hide in my dreams until the dawn of the next day appeared. Yet something was happening on a deeper level. From the subconscious. The human spirit that resides in us all was desperately trying to rise to the occasion.

To quote Jeff Bridges' character in the movie, *Starman:* "You humans are at your very best when things are at their worst."

Is it true? I guess that's for each of us to judge individually. But my opinion tends to be yes. Problem is, many times we can only see that human spirit that was shining through in hindsight. I guess that's because pain can serve as pretty good blinders.

And that pain has lead me to discover something else too: inspiration. Those words that I wrote "X" number of months ago as a release, as an escape, now serve as an inspiration to me. An inspiration to struggle through even the toughest parts life has to offer, to someday look back and learn. Learn from the triumph of overcoming.

An inspiration to write these words for a reason I have yet to know.

ON LIFE

I keep waiting for news to leak out that it's already been secretly approved in France. Hopefully scanning the paper for headlines announcing the start of the FDA's clinical trials. Randomly calling the "carefully selected professionals" from the pages of my health insurance company's directory of managed care providers asking if they dispense it under the counter. But to no avail. On any front. For the magic cure that I seek does not exist. The potent elixir I've hunted my entire life will never be found. Because my quest has revealed there is no vaccination for life. After searching high and low, I've learned that life offers no preventative shot against "bad."

Damn.

Double damn.

It's kind of a letdown, isn't it? I think we all feel a sense of, "If I do this right, live that way and make all the necessary changes, I can pretty much eliminate the uncomfortable parts." Aren't we constantly striving for the secret handshake that will open life's door of happiness forever? Well...sorry. No can do. There are always going to be unpleasant parts. Life can never be "fixed". Never controlled. Never "cured."

It's true. Life is not inherently good or bad. It just must be lived. And that isn't always easy.

That's a hard thing to accept because it leads to a feeling of, "What the hell's the point of trying so hard to get it 'right'?" But I think the way to look at it, to keep from driving yourself crazy, is instead of, "What's the point?" look at it from the perspective, "Hey, life isn't always going to go as planned, or 'right,' so look at the screw ups and unexpected bad parts as part of the plan. The Big Plan."

The more we fight it by not accepting it, the more we add to the pain of the unplanned event. I know that sounds easier in theory than in practice - because it is. But that still doesn't make it any less true. Just look back and test it for yourself. Believe me, I still don't do it enough myself. By a long shot. Hell, if I did, I probably wouldn't be writing this book/journal.

I know that when my friends each would go through some sort of individual and/or personal crisis, I was always the first one there with my little tid-bits of wisdom. Tid-bits that I have yet to use myself. Tid-bits that I think have been passed down from broken dream to broken dream. But does anybody ever test drive these friendly, well-intentioned words of wisdom? Has anybody ever, in the history of mankind, actually tried this crap to see if it works? What if this mish-mash doesn't even remotely "work" (if there is such a word when dealing with human emotions)? How would we know? Can anybody reading this tell me of one friend, one friend of a friend, who followed all the time-honored advice and came through something like this with flying colors? I'd love to meet this person.

My theory is that this stuff probably does and would work, it's just that we can't follow this advice even if we tried. It's impossible. Like some trip switch encoded into our genes. We know it's the right thing to do but the pain of our heart overrides the rationale of our mind. In a battle of the soul, when love is involved, it's simple: Heart > Mind. Kind of like that old rock-paper-scissors game we played as kids. Seems like rock would win all the time. But beware of that paper.

What does this all mean? It isn't as easy as it seems. I guess we just have to each go through the life grinder. Have to. Of course nobody wants to. But think about it. If we all could escape life's pain by following some generation-to-generation, some relationship-to-relationship advice, where would we be as people? Where would our depth, our compassion, our understanding come from? Life is about the experience of living. Good and bad. There are no blueprints. No "just add water" directions.

ON LIFE

It's ironic but the directions and blueprints can only be realized in hindsight and yet, even then, they can't be passed on. Or rather, they can't be heeded at the time of their passing. For there are some things that can only be lived, not "learned" through the words of others who've traveled the path beforehand.

It's one of the great paradoxes and mysteries of...life.

DEFINE "SOON"

Love has no definition but I now think the components that make up love must.

"Someday," "soon" and "before you know it" are handy little phrases and words but they aren't answers. They are excuses. They are excuses when either by choice or ignorance no answer is available. Imagine that you are taking the SAT or some other such standardized test and the following question is posed:

Johnny leaves his house at 9 a.m., has to travel one hour to work, works for 7 hours then takes the long way home which doubles his travel time. What time will Johnny get back home?

Soon.

Chances are, that answer would not and will not get you into the college of your choice. Or maybe it would. That answer might just get you accepted "before you know it."

OLIVE JUICE

WATCH OUT FOR KRYPTONITE

The biggest blunder so many of us make in our personal relationships is thinking they can just be set aside and maintained only when a crisis develops. Like the person who doesn't maintain his car until something goes terribly wrong, the price is much higher than if a little preventative maintenance is used. We need to become maintenance men and not crisis managers in our relationships.

How many of us, when a relationship lay in ruins before our eyes, have said to our friends, "Geez, I don't know what happened. It just came out of the blue."? Chances are it may actually seem that way upon first inspection. Yet upon closer examination, the relational tires were a little low, the brakes were squeaking and the engine had been knocking for a few months now.

It is far too easy to overestimate how much your relationship can take. Even though all the components are (or were) there, every relationship has a breaking point. Every one. Sure, some have much higher tolerance levels and things that would normally wreck most other relationships might not even scratch yours. But don't be fooled just because what ended someone else's relationship had no effect on your situation. Stronger does not mean indestructible. There is a breaking point.

Again - There is a breaking point.

I just feel I should keep saying that over and over again because, even though that has been told to us a thousand times, we often ignore the warnings and keep going on with the status quo, only pulling over when a crisis develops. And while the relationship may still be salvageable, after numerous break-downs, the overall health of the "relationship car" is weakened.

So many of us, when in a loving relationship, feel invincible. Like Superman. And that's great. But remember, even Superman wasn't invincible. Watch out for kryptonite.

I think a lot of that "waiting for the crisis" mentality comes as a result of romance novels or Hollywood ideals of what love actually is. Love is work. It must be "done." While happiness is a feeling we can choose, love is not. It is a result of doing the work. In a movie, it's not fun to watch a man and woman doing the "boring" day-to-day work of maintaining a relationship; it's not cinematically exciting to put on the big screen. That's why the heroes in the movies are always trying to regain lost love. It's exciting and fun to watch for an audience. But it's not fun to live. Do the "boring" work of maintaining your relationship, leave the "exciting" task of regaining love to the movies.

UNDER THE RUG

In my last relationship, we never fought. And I thought that was the coolest thing in the world. To me, that was the sign of the perfect relationship. I'd see all these other couples (many of whom are still together) fighting and think, "Ha! Glad that's not us. We don't fight. Our relationship is great. We don't fight."

ED. NOTE: Please read "fight" here to mean "argue" and not the boxing variety.

But now, looking back with that perfect relationship Monday Morning Spouse Hindsight, I know I was wrong. Not fighting was tantamount to not communicating. Period. I'm not saying you should get into a screaming match every day for the "health" of it. Not at all. What I'm saying is, communication in any loving relationship is a must and since things in life don't always run smoothly, some of that communication is probably going to be uncomfortable in the short term. But the long term benefits far outweigh the short term gains of avoiding the situation.

UNDER THE RUG

Think about any close, loving relationship you have. Be it with parents, siblings, friends, whatever. Is there tension at times? How do you handle it? Most likely, in those above-mentioned situations (especially family, where no matter what, most people know those folks will still be there for them), you have faced that tension - fights if you will - with deep communication and you got through it for the long term benefit of all involved. At the time it might have seemed rough, but looking back, I'll bet you say it was worth it.

Why is it then that so many couples face these tense situations in their relationships by trying to ignore them away? I did that. So many people, myself included, keep the boat steady at communication's expense. And if that cycle goes unchecked, almost always, it will lead to the relationship's downfall. I speak from unwanted experience. We shoved so much stuff under the rug that by the end, we couldn't see each other from across the room.

Seems like there was always "a more appropriate time" to discuss what was bothering me in our relationship. "This isn't the right place," was a common thought in my mind as I debated back and forth whether or not to bring "it" - whatever "it" was - up.

But I've discovered that the appropriate time is now. The right place is right here. Those issues and problems shoved under the rug are the very things that will eventually undermine the entire relationship if not faced head on. I think too often we are scared to bring the thorny issues up out of fear. Fear of what might happen. Fear of the response. Fear of the unknown. Yet, as with all things worthwhile, that fear must be dealt with in order to overcome the obstacles that lead to a healthier relationship tomorrow.

One always thinks, as I did, that to bring up those tough issues instead of just hoping that they'll go away will only lead to greater problems. "Why not just ride it out until the bumps disappear?", the thinking goes. Trouble is, those bumps aren't going to go away unless you clean out from under that rug.

Fear is the worst feeling in the world. Fear of that forever good-bye. But the only way to avoid that fate in the long run is to tackle that fear in the short run, face those issues, bring them up and work them out.

Right now, you yourself might be sitting there thinking, "Yeah, I have some problems that I'd like to talk about with him/her but..."

Forget the "but..." Love is about "and..." Don't wait until the "but..." becomes a forever regret. A never will. An, "I wish." A good-bye.

And what are you thinking now: What if bringing up those issues is what leads to that good-bye? Well, obviously that could happen. But it almost certainly will happen if you don't bring them up. And this will only be after much more pain, heartache and disgust with yourself for not being honest with him/her or yourself.

Spoken like someone who's been there, eh? Well...

Even if the relationship does end, you'll know in your heart of hearts and for the rest of your life that you were honest, not only with that other person, but with yourself. You didn't let your feelings get trampled on while deluding yourself into thinking that you were doing it for the "good" of the relationship.

I hope this is in some way, shape or form clear. I guess all I'm saying is that quite often, it's probably a good idea to get out that relationship broom to do a little sweeping up from underneath that rug. And just like any "house cleaning," it may not be pleasant. It sure won't be fun. Especially in the short run while it is actually happening. But it needs to be done. And should be done on a regular basis. Yet as unpleasant as it all seems right now and during, when the "dust settles," you may just have a whole new, stronger relationship that you didn't even know was possible.

BANDAGE FOR THE HEART

"They say, `War is hell.' Well, so is love. Or at least it's unwanted end. Only there are no medals of honor or purple hearts for bravery - just scars from wounds as seemingly deep and painful as any suffered on the battlefield."

I jotted those words down in my journal, what seems like, a lifetime ago. Hmmm. Got me to thinkin'...

At least we know when physical wounds are healed. The knee doesn't hurt. The arm is not sore to the touch. The cut has closed up. But with wounds of the soul, there is no way to tell upon casual observation. And even when the wound seems healed to the wounded, they can be reopened with ease - a song on the radio, a scent in the air, a moment alone at the park. Any of these and more - the daggers of love.

This entry reminds me, and thus leads me, to a poem I was inspired to write soon after the end of my first serious college relationship. I jotted it down in the library one night while simultaneously studying for some big, important test and wallowing in as much self-pity as I could muster.

...and again

I feel the hurt; the pain is real
A sword's lashing blow -
Yet an aching from within.
No way to duck; not Cain's dagger
An unscathed body to the outer eye -
For the scars are on the soul.

These wounds not measured
As battle's crimson stains
But by the bleeding of tears
From a cut deep inside.
No potions to heal,
No remedies bought or sold,
My only cure being time;
Life's bandage for the heart.

Eric Champnella

Actually, the "bandage for the heart" back then didn't have to be that big or long. I'm much more in need of a tourniquet and emergency room treatment these days. But you know, as I write this, it's kind of neat to look back at those times of such dire distress in one's past and be confronted with a small smile of remembrance where there was once heartache. I have to keep telling myself that today. I'd love to look back on these words someday and wonder what in the hell I thought was so bad that it drove me to write a damn book!

Think about it for a moment. Remember how horrible life seemed when he/she "dumped" you right before prom "X" number years ago? (Or whatever the crisis du jour was back then.) The world stopped spinning, or so it seemed, for a spell. Now doesn't all that seem kind of silly? Maybe that's one of the secrets to life: Don't take it so seriously because just about all of it will eventually bring a smile someday. No matter how bad it seemed at the time.

Yesterday's problems are never as bad tomorrow. And the only way to get to tomorrow is straight through today.

P.S. I can't for the life of me remember how I did on that big, important test back then. Or even what big, important class it was for, for that matter. I only remember the important stuff from that term. The stuff I learned about life. Hmm. I wonder what grade I'm getting in that.

I hope I'm taking the class Pass/Fail.

OLIVE JUICE

THE BALL IS IN YOUR COURT

"The ball is in your court."

I can still hear my girlfriend say those words when she called me out of the blue just over a month after we broke up (notice I say "girlfriend" instead of "ex-girlfriend" because at that time, after six and a half years, I was still trying to get used to the new hyphenated title I would be using to refer to her for the rest of my life).

She had called to say she wanted to be friends. I had not heard a word from her since the break up yet she was calling to see if we could be pals. Chums. Buddies.

Ouch.

Needless to say, with my heart still dangling by a thread, I was not too receptive to such overtures of friendship. Too hard to be "just friends" at that point with the person I thought I was going to grow old with. The person I planned to have children with.

And so I explained this to my Former. That it was just too painful at the time. I still had feelings for her and wasn't even close to being over her or the broken relationship. Maybe somewhere down the road (this weather update just in from southern Hades...).

Yet she couldn't understand this. Thought I was being unreasonable. We had been best friends for so long, she had stated, how was it that we couldn't simply maintain "that" part of our former relationship? Keep that part "alive" while ditching a few minor other parts? I felt like some doctor being asked to take out the patient's heart, brain and lungs - but don't touch the liver! We're saving that so this corpse that was a relationship between these two people can go on and lead a normal and healthy life.

As a friend once told me: You can't break up with someone and hold their hand at the same time. Period.

"Breaking up" means just that. Not "stretching out." Not "expanding apart." Not "fixably split." None of the above. That's why it's called "breaking up." It's broken. It doesn't work anymore.

Don't try and have it both ways. Yes, maybe someday down the road - when you are truly over it - a friendship can ensue. But not before. Not while there are still wounds that can be easily opened.

If you try to force it too soon, be honest, you aren't really trying to be friends. You're really being a "Hey-I'm-Hanging-Around-Trying-To-

See-If-And-Hope-That-You'll-Come-Back-Please-Please-Please" person in her life. And that's not friendship.

As a further test, see how strong that friendship is every time a call is cut short because of "company." Or when the two of you can't get together because of "other plans." That is not friendship. That is painful, self-inflicted surgery that re-opens still-fresh wounds. And believe me, it's surgery without anesthesia.

So I explained the above to my ex, my point-by-point explanation on why we couldn't be friends (although not in so many words. I think I just said something profound like, "Uh, I can't.").

That's when she said it: "Well, you know how I feel. The ball's in your court."

And I was about to hang up. To leave that damn "ball" just sitting there in "my court." But I couldn't let it happen. Wouldn't. This wasn't a basketball game. So I said, "There is no ball and there is no court. Only two people. Me and you. Us."

There was a silence now on the other end of the phone. I was not playing by the "rules" of the "game." I had dissolved the very framework of dealing with the situation. Refused to take the "ball" and be responsible for its safekeeping.

Love is not a sporting event. And a relationship is not a ball that can be conveniently smacked back and forth between the two parties like some tennis match.

It is not a hot potato that can be thrown to the other party when it gets too hot or difficult to handle. Yet, too often that's the way we "play the game."

Love is difficult. Sometimes it gets very "hot" and hard to handle. But instead of something that we must rid ourselves of, think of it as a cherished prize that must be guarded at all costs. A trophy.

You see, love is not the game. That is the "like" stage. The courting. The wooing. That's when things can be tossed back and forth like the above-mentioned tennis match. Because there is no love yet.

But once we get past the "like," past "the game," and into the love, that is the equivalent of the post-game victory celebration. The winners circle. The trophy ceremony. So during the game, while the idea was to blast the ball back and forth all over the court, it all changes in that victorious locker room afterwards. The trophy is yours. The game is over. Hold it high above your head and cherish it.

After hanging up the phone, I felt good. I had gotten rid of that &^%$ ball. But then I had an ironic thought: Since we were no longer in love, at least one of us wasn't, maybe the ball was indeed in my court. It's a cycle...or a season. And I was back at opening day - no, make that spring training. Time to start the games again. Start the process up all over once more.

I guess it was hard to come to grips with that as I sat alone in the locker room of my memories. A place where I was once so recently drenched in the victory champagne of love. But I still believe. Believe that once again I will get to a place where there is no ball and no court. Only two people. Me and you.

A place for us.

OLIVE JUICE

FROM THE JOURNAL

Every now and then it's fun to read something that I thought was so profound when I wrote it only to grimace at how hokey it sounds now. I think the fine line between silly and something that stays with you is your state of mind when you read it. Depends on your mood.

Here are some things that you can probably go either way with. I don't care. It's up to you the reader to take what you get from each - thoughtful smile or shake-of-the-head laugh. Some of you may be moved, others will merely think, "Oh brother." Take your pick.

The Great Discoveries of Life

I find it both sad and amusingly ironic that my break-up has made me grow and reflect on life so much. Sad because it took such heartache to lead to such personal insight and amusing because such insight probably never would've happened without "The Event." It's unfortunate that it takes some great calamity for things like this to occur. Such is the paradox of life.

Why can't I make such realizations after buying a loaf of bread at the grocery store?

Forgive Thyself...

Although I made some huge mistakes, I think it's also time to forgive myself and move on. No more "coulda, shoulda, woulda." Hey, I'm human. We're all bound to make them. I can't crucify myself forever for them. Time to try to put those things/thoughts in my past.

On Forgetting...Again

Have to simply "let" myself move on. Trying to move on is like trying not to think of the proverbial pink elephant. No luck.

A Book?

Thinking about starting a book with all this stuff in it. For who? I guess for anyone who has ever gone through this. If I can ease, or at least comfort, one person who is going through this, then it would be worth the effort. I just need to pick myself up enough to do it.

Looking the Wrong Way

I keep looking at the sunset waiting for the sun to rise.

IN THE LAND OF DINOSAURS

I used to always say to people who broke up, "There's always someone else." It was my pat answer. Didn't care what the situation was. Nor just how special the now-former had been. Don't bother me with specifics. You want my opinion? Don't worry because:

There's always someone else. Period.

Well, now that I've been on the other end of that advice, I can honestly say with all certainty that I'm quite surprised I never got my ass kicked. I'm kind of mildly shocked I didn't suffer at least one quick shot to the head. Slightly relieved I didn't get an unexpected jab to the solar plexus. I feel this now because these are the absolute last words one wants to hear in that situation. No matter how true and how well meaning the advice, save it for later.

Even in the worst of personal worst times, I knew in my mind that my oft-given words of reassurance were true but my heart just didn't believe. And let's face it, at those moments of deep personal distress, the "Mind" is a second class citizen to the needs, whims and reasoning of the "Heart."

My blinded sense of logic at the time went something like this: What if I lucked out and found The One my first time? What if I found my "someone else" on the very first try? Uh-oh.

So, as each of my well-meaning friends told me the same thing I had probably told all of them at one point in their own lives, I politely nodded my head. All the while focusing on their exposed solar plexus region.

It's not that I didn't, on some level, buy these dreaded words. That's not even the point. The point is I didn't care. We all don't care right about then. It doesn't matter if there are 100 someone elses out there just waiting in a big line at the front door. We don't want "someone else" at that point in time. We want the person who has just ripped our heart out and left us for dead by the side of the relationship highway. Like some emotional road kill. (It's ironic but when my friends told me that this imaginary "someone else" would be ten times better than my ex, I didn't want this near-perfect mirage. I wanted the highly non-perfect person who had just gutted me. Go figure. I guess a heartbreaker in the hand is worth two angels in the bush.)

But you know what? There always is someone else. There has to be. If not, we, the human race, would cease to exist. If there was only one, and the feeling of "never again like that one" stayed with us; if the thought of eternal loneliness we each feel after the loss of true love held true and did indeed keep us alone, then the human race would eventually fade away. Would have a long time ago.

Dinosaurs must've had only one true love.

OLIVE JUICE

LIFE LESSONS

I must state right off, before you start to read this, that I've never been much of a man of science. Too many facts. Too concrete. Too black and white. Not enough room for change. And quite honestly, too much damn homework in high school. Or more appropriately stated: too much hard homework in high school.

For me, it was always much easier to b.s. my way through an essay question. I always figured if I wrote long enough, strung enough cool sounding sentences together, somewhere in between the pages of my bluebook would lie the semblance of an answer that would keep my academic career chugging along. But such wordplay, I had discovered long ago, didn't cut it in math or the other hard sciences. Let's face it, there is really no way to bluff your way through a calculus mid-term. The answer was the answer. Period. You either knew it or you didn't. And to be honest, most of the time, I didn't. Hell, they didn't even have bluebooks.

Therefore, I always seemed to take the path of books and words over numbers and facts (which is probably best for all of us right now. Believe me, you would definitely NOT be reading anything I had written about Pythagoras). So, with that little piece of background info, it may strike you as strange that I would like to venture into the realm of science here. But I have a hypothesis I'd like to run by you. Call it Champnella's First Theorem.

Before I state my theory, it must all be noted that the extensive research and testing that has gone into "proving" my postulate is really quite limited. It's based on my own personal experiences and the accounts of those dear to me. Yet, I'm starting to believe it with all the certainty of a chemical equation. That's because I, and probably most of you reading this, have done better than proven it in a laboratory. We've each lived it. And to me, that's case closed. Don't need any further research. Keep your grant money. Those who need more may call it a hunch, I call such things Life Lessons.

My hypothesis deals with the human heart. You see, like those who thought the sun revolved around the earth and others who believed the earth was flat, I think modern science might just be a little off about the heart. We've been told all our lives that the heart is a pumping station for the human body. The Grand Central Station of our arteries. But is that all? Is our heart just some highly efficient sump pump? Sure, if we base our findings on the strictly medical. Yet, maybe conventional science is all wrong. Maybe our current levels of advancement don't quite allow us to see the whole picture. So I'd like to question conventional wisdom on the heart with my own little theory. A theory that quite possibly could've gotten me burned at the stake a couple hundred years ago when disagreeing with "science" and "facts" was seen in a much less forgiving light. But luckily nowadays I'll probably fair no worse than being dismissed as a hopeless romantic.

So here goes: I think the heart is more. More than a pipeline. More than the body's main blood interchange. I strongly believe that we can actually "think" with our hearts. Just as certainly as we can figure out those annoying calc problems with our mind, we can also figure out problems just as complex using the "thinking" mechanism we each have in our hearts.

Now don't get me wrong, I'm not disavowing the thinking done by the mind. I'm merely putting forth that we have a choice. A choice between the heart and the mind when it comes to making a decision. In fact, there are some things we probably couldn't "think" through using the heart. Like those calculus problems for example. Rather, the heart is made for "thinking" through and deciding specific problems dealing with issues which affect the heart itself the most: life and love. Yet, too often, we still use the mind for solving these problems which are more suited toward solutions from the heart.

I think if the problem affects the heart, the solution itself should come from the heart as well. Makes sense doesn't it? If you're dealing with a broken heart, who should best know how to fix it, the heart or the mind? That's why I truly believe the heart has some special capacity that no medical text or science book tells us about that actually allows it to "think" to help solve the problems that specifically deal with its well being.

While growing up, either by plan or genetics, it seems we come to almost always use the mind when deciding. We're told to "think it all the way through," "to make up your mind," and to "use your head." So naturally, the thinking process of the heart takes a permanent backseat.

But I feel there are many times, in dealing with some of life's toughest questions, when we shouldn't be rational or use logic to solve a problem. When our thinking caps should be left in the corner. At these times, and I can't tell you which times these are (that being one of your first tests of this theory), it's best to go with your gut instinct, to "follow your heart." For, has anyone ever been led astray who truly and honestly followed their heart? I haven't. Yet too often, we don't. Following your heart is sometimes the dangerous option. The risky choice. The road less traveled.

This isn't to say that following the "thinking" of your heart will lead to success in whatever you were doing or wanted. But, I can almost guarantee that it will lead to personal satisfaction that you did the right thing. That you took the path and chose the side that was truest to your spirit.

How many times have you heard the phrase, "you're thinking too much?" Which side do you suppose they're talking about? Certainly not the heart. That's when you have to throw caution to the wind and follow the decision that has been made inside your heart.

The mind always seems to have a wealth of "logical" avenues with which to solve our problems of love and life, yet the heart usually only has one option. You can tell which one is from your heart, too. It's the one that just feels right inside. The one that you might have a hard time explaining to your friends about why. The one that you should probably just follow.

And who knows, maybe when we do start thinking with our hearts instead of our minds, maybe then will we start to shed some of our human toils. For I truly believe that God thinks with His heart. That's because, while church, family and society may put God in our minds, He can only be found in our hearts.

So next time, take a chance. Don't wait for the logical part of you to figure it all out. You can't. That's part of life. Follow your heart. Trust it. Listen to it. You just may be surprised at the result.

It's all true. I read it in a science book somewhere. Some proven Theorem.

OLIVE JUICE

POEMS AND THOUGHTS

About a month and a half after *The Crisis* (see page 19), I got the urge to start writing poetry again. I literally hadn't written anything poetic since college but somehow I felt the need once more.

The first result was the poem on the following page.

FOR A MOMENT

Thinking for a moment
Of words that tell thee
Not of merely spoken,
But from Life's heart
Of thoughts I dare express.

Hoping for a moment
The child's eyes shine blue,
Which I'd sworn stolen
From the heavens. Alas,
A glance confirms new skies.

Pausing for a moment
In memory's vast expanse,
I sit quietly watching.
Lost between the trees of was
And the streams of nevermore.

Wishing for a moment
To snatch time's unseen hand;
Still cursing fate's reward
At destiny's taken path.
For want of a kiss good-bye.

Finally stopping for a moment,
Mindful of yesterday's demise,
I search out forward
Waiting for the epiphany -
The reveal of a sequestered tomorrow.

Eric Champnella

Just reading it again puts me in a trance-like state. It gets me thinking about life again. I guess that's what one hopes any poem he writes does to someone who reads it - either gets them to think or makes them feel something. To me personally, this poem actually does both. I wonder if half of it is simply because it takes me back to another time in my life. Yet even more than that, or rather, more simply than that, this poem makes me smile. I can't help but feel optimistic after I read it. It just kind of makes me want to plow through the toughest parts of today to get to the surprise of an unknown tomorrow.

I hope when you read this, it put a smile on your face as well. I'm sure Whoever passed it on to me would've wanted it that way.

OLIVE JUICE

STARING INTO THE FACE OF GOD

"The south rim of the Grand Canyon.

Wow!!!! This is the single most incredible natural wonder I've ever seen in my life. I just saw the Canyon for the first time about 5 minutes ago. I wish I had all day to sit here and write. This is the most inspiring thing/place I've ever seen in my 27 years.

Even if you're not religious, you can't help but feel something. Like Megan said, `It's like staring into the face of God.'

To put it mildly.

I actually felt my pulse quicken when I looked out for the first time and saw the magnitude of what lay before me. I don't have a camera with me so these words will have to be the pictures for my mind to look back on in the future."

Those words started out my journal entry one August day when I gazed out over the Grand Canyon for the very first time. As you can tell from the above, it's an experience one does not soon forget. My friend wasn't too far off when she said it was like staring into the face of God.

I arrived at the Canyon late in the afternoon, yet I still managed to hit every viewing area along the south rim. Even if the next one was only a couple hundred yards up the road, with no real sightline differences, I didn't want to take the chance of missing anything. Too beautiful an opportunity to let slip away. Didn't want to pass up even the chance of something.

The Canyon had a strange effect on the people there as well. I know this may sound corny, but it seemed to make everyone "friendlier." Sure, there is always the possibility that I just happened to make my stop on a day when the park was overrun with a multitude of particularly friendly people, but I don't think that was the case. I think the Canyon has a mystical effect on those who view and possess its beauty before them. I think it would be impossible to feel hate or anger or contempt toward another person as you stood at the Canyon. One can't help but just feel joy. Joy at being a part of that whole crazy adventure we call the human race. That doesn't make it any easier, but somehow it makes one feel that you'll at least be able to get through the tough parts.

The Canyon to me is a great equalizer. Nobody is better or worse than anyone else as you stand before it. We are all one. One piece of a much bigger Picture that created the Canyon in the first place. Gazing out into the Canyon, I couldn't help but feel like a very small piece in that Picture. Somehow, looking out at the magnitude before me made everything else seem almost trivial. In two hundred years, was any of what I was going through really going to matter? Probably not. So why worry myself to death over it. Hell, chances are in two years it wasn't going to matter. Maybe even shorter than that.

Now, obviously, this state of utter peace only lasted for the time which I spent at the Canyon rim. But the thing was, it happened. If only for a second. If only for a moment. It was possible, even for the briefest duration, for there to be peace within once again. To feel actual happiness. Wow.

I'm not saying one has to travel to the Grand Canyon to find tranquility and happiness when going through one of life's toughest challenges (although if you can, I can't recommend it highly enough. Like a mother's kiss on a skinned knee as a small child, it makes it all feel better!). I'm just letting you know that there even exits that tranquility within - at a time when it seems impossible.

And when you can feel that, even for a millisecond, somehow you just know it's going to be all right. Because there was recently a time when that very millisecond felt like an eternity of pain. So while it may not last very long when you first start to feel it again, just knowing it can be there once more makes everything seem just a little bit better.

STARING INTO THE FACE OF GOD

I must share with you one other final experience regarding my trip to the Grand Canyon. As I wound my way along the south rim, I made it to the eastern-most viewing area just as the last vestiges of light streaked across the summer sky.

Trudging out of my car, I passed scores of people getting ready to witness the awesome spectacle about to take place: a sunset over the Grand Canyon.

People carried their cameras and camcorders toward the ridge, getting ready to forever capture and record this once in a lifetime sight. Fathers carried their children. Couples walked arm in arm. You could almost feel something in the air. From above, our single-minded trek to the edge must have looked like the epic final scene from a movie of Ben Hur proportions.

Arriving at the viewing area, I settled myself in on the rock against the wooden observation tower. The sunset was only minutes away now. Next to me, a couple from Germany lay in each other's arms against a tree as he readied his Pentax. Catching my smiling glance, a small nod came my way.

To the other side of me, a father sat with his young daughter on a small bench. The well-worn bench had the engravings of hundreds of other couples who had come before to watch the nearing sight. Their own yearnings at immortality via the bench slowing being forever washed away by the other etchings of daily visitors and by Nature itself.

In front of me against the rail stood an elderly couple, his hands gingerly placed against her shoulders. Every few moments a gentle kiss would find its way to the small of her neck. They looked so enthralled with each other, this could've even been their first date. But the touches of familiarity and the rings on each hand said otherwise. (I've always been inspired by older couples in love. It seems so genuine. Like they've figured it all out and now there's nothing left to do but enjoy the secret. Time becoming their ally in further strengthening the bonds of love as each moment passes.)

The sunset was now only moments away. The Pentax whirred into action, capturing the "just before" pictures. The father helped his daughter stand on the once-painted bench to get the best possible view. And the hands of the elderly couple clasped together, as I'm sure had been done a thousand times over the years. Here it comes...

And then I walked away.

I got up, brushed myself off and smiled at the obviously puzzled German couple. I turned around and headed toward the parking lot, passing a few stragglers who were rushing over to get to the edge before the show began. Reaching my car, I got in and drove away.

A few minutes later, driving from the Canyon to continue my journey, I could see the sun beginning to set in my rearview mirror.

"God, it must be beautiful there along the edge," I thought to myself as I headed east.

Heading toward tomorrow.

You see, I wasn't running from the sight I had just left, I was saving it. Saving a sunset for someone I don't even know yet. So I can give it away as a small little gift. A small treasure from my heart for the person I have yet to meet but I know is out there somewhere.

So as I continued east, the glare of the past reflecting in my eyes off the mirror, I caught a small glimpse of the future. My future. And I saw a camera in my hands as I lay against the tree. A child's tug against my sleeve as I held her close atop the bench. A small kiss upon my weathered cheek as I stood beside the railing.

Then in my mind's eye I saw the sun set across the Canyon for the very first time. The sunset I had passed on today but was saving for tomorrow. As I stood with someone yet to know, staring into the face of God.

THE LITTLE THINGS OF LOVE

"You may never, due to things said or events passed, call me again. I understand. If not, remember me, not for the big dreams that got away, but for the small moments we shared. A laugh at a football game. A kiss on the forehead. A warm smile caused by a Diet Coke at a gas station.

The little things of no reason save love."

Those words were part of a last-ditch letter I wrote to my old girlfriend trying in vain to save our forever-shattered relationship. It was over. I "knew" it in my head but couldn't get the reality relay to work for my heart. Since the break up had been over the phone, I was still needing a face-to-face encounter to get it through my sometimes-thick head that the end was upon us (Maybe I should've written it 1,000 times on a blackboard just to get it to sink in; like elementary school teachers used to make those of us who were much too talkative in class write, "I will be quiet" in second grade to get a point to stick. Hmm.

Interesting concept).

Anyway, while the letter didn't "work" in terms of getting us back together, I still believe in the wisdom of those words.

"The little things of no reason save love."

Too often, I think we only see love in terms of the movies:

FADE IN:

EXT. ROMANTIC PARK SETTING - DUSK

ANGLE ON A HORSE-DRAWN CARRIAGE

as it slowly makes it way toward the center of the park. Two people sit inside.

We HEAR the SWEEPING MUSICAL SCORE as we

ZOOM IN ON OUR HERO AND HEROINE

inside the carriage. They embrace and gaze into each other's eyes before both getting swept up in the moment. Finally, they kiss each other with the most passion they have ever felt as the SWEEPING MUSICAL SCORE reaches a crescendo.

As they continue to kiss we...

FADE OUT:

THE END

ROLL CREDITS

Trouble with that scenario is, there are no credits in real life. Love is so much more than that by showing itself in so many less obvious ways. Unfortunately, it took a whole heck of a lot of pain for me to figure that out myself. I kept waiting for the sweeping musical score to announce the beginning of the "happily ever after" credits. But I suppose that's the way it is with most people. We're forever waiting for the big realization. Forever waiting for the time when everything just "falls into place" and the "happily ever after" part starts. Forever waiting for "The Moment."

But you know what? The Moment never comes. That's not what love is. While we spend our days endlessly waiting and looking for this big bolt of lightening, we end up missing the best parts. The little things of no reason save love.

Love doesn't need a grand entrance to show itself. Love doesn't need trumpets to announce its comings and goings. Love doesn't wait for a "more perfect time" or bigger arena before making its presence known. When love appears, it is just there. All around.

I think next time, now that I know this, hopefully I will start to live it to the fullest. I've stopped waiting for the big moments and I've learned to not only enjoy, but cherish the small ones. For their sum is The Moment. The Moment is plural. It is the compilation of all the little ones. We don't have just one great and final realization, rather we have a lifetime of them. One on top of the other. We just have to pay attention so as not to let them go unnoticed.

Look around you. Look inside you. They are there. In a laugh. In a kiss. In a smile. You won't even need the big moments anymore. You'll be too busy enjoying the so-called small ones.

OLIVE JUICE

"Olive Juice."

Have you ever heard that phrase between couples? My girlfriend and I used to say that to each other all the time. It meant, "I love you."

I don't remember its origins between us. I honestly don't even know how it got started in general. I think it was an old high school saying. Apparently, somebody once noticed that if you mouthed the words, "Olive juice," the lips looked like they were forming the words, "I love you." And so it became our own cute little declaration of affection. Patrick Swazye and Demi Moore had "Ditto" in the movie "Ghost," we had "Olive juice."

(Warning: After you read this, if you've never heard of that expression before, I can almost guarantee that you will either head straight for the nearest mirror or to your loved one to verify the "Olive Juice" test for yourself. If you use the mirror, make sure no one is standing behind you as you check the accuracy of what I've said.

Believe me, it might be a bit hard to explain to a friend why you're mouthing, "I love you" to yourself in the bathroom mirror.)

"Olive juice" was perfect for parties or other crowded places where the outward display of love and the like might not be appropriate. Those words were kind of like a nice little stop-gap measure until the "real" words could be uttered at a later time. An emotional band-aid if you will.

We each couldn't help but smile when the other person said it. Especially around people who had no idea. It was our secret. Something we shared between us. And isn't that what love is all about?

Sometimes, we would even have the other person try and guess which of the two phrases we were really saying as one of us mouthed either "Olive juice" or "I love you." Even though they both stood for the same thing, it was just one of those homemade, improvised little games we all play when we are in love. After a while, we both got pretty good at it. Each of us could spot a bogus "I love you" disguised as "Olive juice" a mile away.

When someone would catch us using our little saying, we would try and explain it to them if they asked. And more often than not, they would look at us like we were just a tad unglued. Oh, sure, they'd nod and smile like they "got it" but you could see the truth of the matter in their eyes. That made us laugh and grin even more. They wouldn't get it if we sat down and drew out a diagram. The only way to understand is to be there yourself. You call it crazy, I call it being in love.

Poets, artists and all of us have been trying since the beginning of man to explain love, yet I don't think anyone has nailed down the definitive answer. It's still the greatest of mysteries and probably always will be. I think that's half the beauty of love. There is no answer. It can never be solved. It can only be lived.

Now, looking back on that relationship that is no more, the cynic in me occasionally thinks, "Hmm. Maybe she was just saying `Olive juice' after all." But, thankfully, that quickly passes and I'm able to see through the residual pain. I'm able to see those words for what they really were at one time in my life.

You see, besides being convenient, "Olive juice" stood for something else. Something special. It was a bond. It was the way two people, who have been together a very long time, can let the other person know just how much they care without any effort. Without "trying." It's when you can give away your whole heart with just a touch. Just a glance. Just a silly little saying.

I don't say "Olive juice" anymore these days. I haven't found that next person yet. And when I do, I probably won't use the words "Olive juice" either. That's from the past. Something and someone else. But I will say it again. It may be in a totally different phrase. A special look. A secret wink. Yet, in whatever form, it will still mean the same as "Olive juice" once did. In a different time. In a different place.

And "Olive juice" means "I love you."

THE STAGES

1) Denial and Isolation
2) Anger
3) Bargaining
4) Depression
5) Acceptance

Many people are familiar with the above. They are Elizabeth Kubler-Ross' 5 stages of the grieving process people go through when they discover they have a terminal illness.

Well, the end of a serious relationship is pretty tough in its own right. Not to say that the two such events are in any way equals. Although sometimes a break-up sure seems like a death. It certainly feels like the death of a lot of dreams, hopes and aspirations. It's end of the line for a terminal disease called love.

That's why, after much scientific research (i.e. - talking to my friends) and evaluation (i.e. - writing it down at this particular moment) with a tad of imagination thrown in (i.e. - I'm making this stuff up), I've observed and am here to report on the process that we all go through after the bitter and unexpected end of a serious long-term relationship (i.e. - when you get dumped!). What, for lack of a better term (and because I wrote this book), I'll simply call Eric Champnella's 5 Stages of Dealing With Getting Your Heart Ripped Out and Being Emotionally Left for Dead. Otherwise known as Champ's 5 Stages of D. with G.Y.H.R.O. & B.E.L.F.D. for short.

Now these stages closely follow Kubler-Ross' five, but stray off in a couple of key areas. Hopefully by putting them down here on paper for you, it will help you to closely chart and follow your own course as you sail those often-choppy relationship waters.

The First Stage: *Telecommunications and "Blinking"*

The body's first natural response after getting dumped is to immediately turn toward technology for answers and to soothe initial pain. In other words: Waiting for that &*%$^@> phone to ring.

"Any second now she's going to call back, right?"

"It's got to be close to April 1, doesn't it?"

"Maybe the ringer is turned off..."

Guess again.

Working closely in tandem with that &*%$^@> phone is the now-dreaded answering machine (or non-answering machine as you will soon find out), now the most vile of all human creations. A modern symbol of what happens when man doesn't adequately know the destructive power and potential behind today's scientific advances. When technology out paces wisdom. A modern-day version of Frankenstein.

As you pass through this initial stage, you will come to dread, despise and hate that damn red "blink" on your answering machine. It will come to symbolize all things evil in the known universe. And God help you if you have the ability to check your answering machine remotely (No, it's not broken!).

The Second Stage: *Stuff*

Over the course of a serious long-term relationship (long enough that you're going through "stages" and possibly reading these with a tad more seriousness than was initially intended), you'll notice that your once-significant other has acquired a lot of your things over the years. Some of them will be items you can't even name. Others will be prized possessions: your favorite WHAM! CD, your treasured ticket stub from the '84 NFC title game, your cherished KISS/Cheap Trick World Tour concert t-shirt. In other words, most of the good stuff.

Once you've stopped cursing the answering machine long enough to realize you're missing family heirlooms, you'll have entered stage number two - Stuff. Or more appropriately: I want my stuff back.

It's not even the re-acquisition of your belongings that fuels the emotions in this tough second stage. It's the feeling that the entire relationship itself was just one big elaborate scheme to rob you of your worldly goods. To keep you and the melodic croonings of George Michael forever separated from one another. The audacity!

Actually obtaining your stuff back presents quite a quandary. How do you do it? How do you let the ex know its time to relinquish the jewels? Phone call? Registered mail? Stuck-in-the-middle third party? These are all important decisions that must be taken into consideration during Stage Two.

And one final note of caution regarding the Stuff Stage. While he/she has gobs of your stuff, it only stands to reason that you have come into "ownership" of a lot of his/her stuff. This is where an amazing double standard becomes evident. Because, while you obviously consider your things sacred and untouchable during its "captivity" by the ally-turned-enemy, like relationship POWs protected by the Breaking Up Rules of Engagement as ratified by the Geneva Convention, his/her things enjoy no such refuge. While the very thought of your KISS shirt being treated with anything less than the shielded status it deserves is tantamount to a hostile act of war, his/her things are fair game. As a matter of fact, don't be surprised if that picture she gave you in her favorite frame doesn't survive the first night air strikes of the break up. An unfortunate victim of unexplained collateral damage. And that favorite sweatshirt he forgot last time he stayed over? Forget it. Those types of things have a tendency to be destroyed by friendly fire. Or at least end up as dust rags.

So, the point is, remember to get your stuff back first before intelligence reports confirm the destruction of her stuff. Such disclosures could lead to the need for a heck of a lot of tape to repair that ticket stub.

The Third Stage: *Phil Collins*

Ok. You're sitting around your house with all your stuff back. You're wearing your KISS t-shirt and the ticket stub is safely back in the junk drawer in your kitchen. Life should be good. But somehow it still isn't all right. Something is still missing. Every time you hear "Wake Me Up Before You Go-Go" you begin to get all misty eyed. And not just because of Andrew Ridgley's haunting vocals. Uh-oh, get ready for Stage Three.

The early symptoms of this stage are your thoughts and desires to contact the ex one last time. No one reason. No single thing. Just some unexplainable urge. A last minute hope that all can actually be saved. An eleventh hour reprieve if you will. (Not that you need her or this relationship. But you just don't want to see her make a mistake that she will regret for the rest her life. Remember, you are simply doing your humanitarian duty.)

The only problem is, by this time, there's a good chance that you haven't seen the ex since the exchange of possessions at the Brandenburg break-up bridge. Mainly because she has gone on with her life as you continue to wallow in a sea of self-pity. Ok, that coupled with the fact that when you did see each other for the last time at the drop zone, she was none too thrilled to find out about the mass destruction of her belongings. Picky, picky, picky.

So right about now, your only connection with her might be the now-familiar (and more often than not, memorized) outgoing message on her machine. Your last link. The Alaskan pipeline of fading love.

Of course it must be noted here that you could be getting her machine, not because she's not there, but because she is screening her calls to avoid you in the first place. But that's beside the point

Once you stop wondering and trying to analyze if she really is as happy as she sounds on that new outgoing message, you now decide to use the technology to your advantage. One last ditch effort to revive the relationship vital signs and renew your faith in the peaceful uses of answering machines.

After a couple of pleading messages left on her machine, kind of as a test the waters maneuver, it is time to resort to the meat and potatoes of Stage Three when she doesn't return those calls. (And, yes she got your messages. Just as your machine wasn't broken in Stage One, hers works just fine in Stage Three.) The various components of Stage Three are as follows: 1) Call her up. 2) Patiently wait for that way-too-chipper-to-be-true outgoing message to end. (Who's she trying to kid anyway?) 3) Wait for the beep. 4) Play that old "One More Night" song by Phil Collins over and over again. 5) When she still doesn't call back, repeat.

The Fourth Stage: *Bushes, Blinds and Binoculars*

Ok, she has a new unlisted phone number. Welcome to the end of the third stage and the beginning of the fourth: Stalking.

Once you've confirmed with the operator that her new number is indeed not in the phonebook (you've given her every conceivable spelling and misspelling - including all Pig Latin variations), Stage Four symptoms usually begin to show themselves. Right about here, a couple of unannounced visits to her friends, family and place of employment should be just enough to get you one final (and irate!) message on your machine. (Hey, if she hadn't gone and had her number changed in the first place, this wouldn't have happened would it! Just goes to show - once again - whose fault this all is. But you're such a giver, you won't hold this against her and will continue to try and patch things up. What a guy!)

As you replay in your mind all the things that went wrong and figure out that maybe you were just a tad (half a tad) wrong when you accidentally dropped her picture frame while gathering her things to return to her, Stage Four occupants will usually try many different approaches at contact. "If I could just explain..." is a commonly uttered phrased in Stage Four. (That "dot-dot-dot" part after "explain" is not an unfinished thought due to space constraints in this book, but rather that is usually the point where the door gets slammed in your face.)

Stage Four is usually the briefest of all the stages for, if it is followed too long or too ardently, it could lead, not to Stage Five, but to an undesirable offshoot of Stage Four: Temporary Restraining Order.

The Fifth Stage: *Friends*

"Boy, some people just take things too seriously and blow them way out of proportion. Thank goodness for legal counsel. What did I see in her anyway?"

Truer words were never spoken. Here's to Stage Five. The End of the Line. You're finally over her. Called "Acceptance" in the "other" 5

Stages, but named here after the main tenant and sign of that acceptance, the last leg of the final part of the odyssey: Dating Her Best Friend.

What the hell. It's not like we're seeing each other anymore. Funny how things work out for the best, eh?

Oh, and hey, it has nothing to with revenge or anything like that. It's just that, over the course of your ordeal, you come to realize that that initial attraction you felt to her childhood pal (the one who was going to be "Maid of Honor" in your wedding) had nothing to do with the mass quantities of alcohol you consumed at the party that night after all. It was merely the true feeling of romance expressing itself the best way it knew how at that particular moment.

Yeah. Besides, she said once before that she loves WHAM!. Man, if only they would do that big reunion tour that the press keeps teasing us with. It would cement everything.

And just think, if things go as well with her best friend as they did with your ex-girlfriend, by the time you get to Stage Five next time, you'll be back with your initial old girlfriend. Get it? It's kind of like looking into a mirror of looking into a mirror. The ultimate relationship mind puzzle.

Ah, love.

OLIVE JUICE

ROSE-COLORED GLASSES

I sit and write these words about the past with a heart that is both tempered and untouched by time. Both healed and still wounded. Wiser by truth and taunted by memory. For I look back with a sometimes-curse: The rose-colored glasses of a broken heart.

With these glasses, I have the power to change the past. But not how you may think. Not by going back and reliving it. Not via time capsule or other option so sci-fi. For you do not re-live the past, rather you re-invent the past. In your mind's eye. Here's how...

Not long after my girlfriend and I broke up, someone asked me this question as I lamented the loss of Perfect Love:

"Are you mourning a fantasy?"

"What does that mean?" I inquired.

"Well, it just seems that the relationship you miss is better than the one you once told me about."

Hmm. I didn't know how to answer that.

There was definitely some validity to that observation. But my first instinct was to defend myself. I wasn't mourning a fantasy. What if I was simply now realizing what got away? That there is no movie-ending romance in the real world?

And yet...

It's a fine line between the relationship that was and the one that might have been. A fine line that's hard to distinguish with a heart in distress. The sometimes curse of the rose-colored glasses when seen through a broken heart.

And I don't know about you, but I don't only remember in "fact." I also remember in "feeling." While fact is the basis for the memories, those facts are well colored and shaded with heavy doses of "feeling." That's why, right after a tumultuous break up, that now-passed relationship looks so much better than, in all actuality, it probably was. Missing not what we had or lost, but what we thought we had or think we have now lost for the future.

Mourning for a "fantasy" due to the Sometimes Curse.

I say "sometimes curse" because, on one hand, the great thing about looking at the past through rose-colored glasses is that, down the road, we get to control the strength of the prescription. When the pain of the end of forever now brings a small smile. When the despair over fallen promises is now barely recognizable. When the tears from vanquished dreams are now a passing thought before sleep.

But the bad thing is, sometimes we can't. Not right away at least. Sometimes the hurt gets the best of us. Sometimes it's still just too hard. When the joy felt at "forever's" first utterance is now replaced by the an almost dull throbbing - the bittersweet taste of yearning. Not for what was, but for what might have been.

Ouch. The Curse.

I've at least figured out that the only antidote for this curse is time. I know, I know. I wish there was some quick fix myself. Some pill. Hell, even contacts instead of these damn rose-colored glasses.

But nope. Only time.

You know the expression, "Time heals all wounds?" As I sit here and write, I got to thinking, "Yeah, but how?" Here's my theory: Time heals all wounds because Time has the ability to brighten our memory. To literally shade the dark edges with a ray of sunshine and light that wasn't there when the initial event took place.

In some ways, for comparison's sake, it's almost like looking back many years later on your high school or college days. There's a reason so many people look back on those moments as "the best four years of my life." It's because those memories have been colored by time. Not that those days, weeks and years weren't great and shouldn't be remembered as such, it's just that we look back now and see them as even better than they actually were. When looking back at their high school and college days, nobody seems to remember the number of times they and their friends said something to the effect, "Man, I can't wait to get the hell out of here."

I think many people look back with a wistful eye at the past and a wary one toward the future because in hindsight, it (the past) was survived. Plain and simple. Black and white. We made it through so it couldn't have been that bad in the first place. Yet, the future... Now that's scary, because maybe, just maybe, we won't make it through.

There are no guarantees from the unknown.

I also think a lot of this wistful yearning has to do with the fact that we can't get whatever it was back. Something that is gone forever, even though not perfect (not even close) the first time around, is remembered much better than something we can do or get again. Let's face it, who would want to go back to those awkward 16 year old days if they REALLY, HONESTLY could? Seriously. I don't think too many of us really would if actually possible. But we can't so it looks so much better in the cravings of the impossible.

Nobody yearns with regret for an attainable (or rather RE-attainable) goal. Only the untouchable.

And so for those who say we can't change the past, I say you are wrong. It can be changed. Frequently is changed - In your mind. As now-shaded memory. Those who say you can't change the past have never looked back with heartbreak.

So we are forced to wear our rose-colored glasses. It's just the way it is I guess. Casting the wistful glance ever backward and a wary one cautiously forward. But not forever. For someday the past becomes not a burden, but a fading memory...not in importance but in ability to continue to hurt. The balance gradually shifted between staring back and peeking ahead, ever so slowly, over time, until the Curse is lifted.

OLIVE JUICE

A POEM

Below is an untitled poem I wrote. I figured the above entry just kind of naturally lead to this next piece.

`Tis cruelest of Love's fleeting
Thine squandered vision
When, deeper into past facades,
Now's mem'ries so perfect
To the essence of yore,
Guide thee to reconstruct.
Not from truth's vantage
But false sightings of was,
Leading thee to look west
For the dawn of tomorrow new;
Forever's vanquish thus heightened
With mournings for not.

Eric Champnella

OLIVE JUICE

THE STATUS QUO

Some recently told me that relationships are never standing till. Never static. They are either moving forward or backwards. Growing or dying.

How true.

I guess I used to think that, in some ways, relationships could be put on hold or "paused." Like a VCR or Super Nintendo. But that just isn't the case. There is no hold button on love. Only a forward and a reverse. A cue and a rewind. A coming or going.

I wish I'd understood this a long time ago. Before it was too late. Because, as I think back to all the times when I said and thought to myself that my old relationship was in a rut, or kind of at a stand still, or just wasn't going anywhere, I now realize that I was wrong. The relationship indeed was going somewhere. Unfortunately, unknown to me at the time, it was backwards. My relationship was dying and I didn't even see it. That realization hurts just as much as anything. That I could be so blind. So naive to something that supposedly was so very important to me.

And I'm probably not the only one.

I say all this because some of you, if not many of you, reading this book may now be in the same boat I was in. If you are, get out! "Danger! Danger, Will Robinson!" Look at the name on the side of that boat. I think it says, "Titanic."

If I may give you just one piece of unwanted firsthand knowledge, it's that love doesn't sit on the sidelines; love is always in the game. You may think that love is just kind of hanging out while your relationship hits a snag. Just kind of waiting around while things hang in limbo. But, sad to say, you are wrong. Sorry to be the bearer of bad news.

For love waits not for a better time. Love knows not a more appropriate opportunity. Love cannot stand still. Love lives only in the here and now. Love is alive. And if love stands still, it begins to perish.

You see, love is too precious to just sit around. Too cherished and yearned for by so many others to stay in a holding pattern where it is not being fully appreciated. So if left unattended, if left without nurture, love will fade away. That's because love is not passive. Love must be "used." Love has to be "done."

In the sentence "I love You," guess which word is the verb? Guess which word you have to "do?"

So "do" love.

THE STATUS QUO

AUTHOR'S NOTE: Notice how I don't say the oft-mentioned, "Love is hard work." That's due to the fact that, because "work" seems to have such a negative connotation in our society, I don't want to give the impression that maintaining your relationship is like digging ditches. While it's definitely not easy and always involves sacrifice, love is not a punishment. Love is not a chore. Love is not work - at least not in the negative sense you probably view the thing and/or place you have to get up for at 6:30 a.m. tomorrow. Rather, love is a treasure. And while you may have to dig for it, that only makes it more valuable. If it was just sitting there, how much would we truly appreciate it? So how could that be called "hard work?"

Now, what do you do if your current relationship is stuck in one of those ruts? I wish I had the answer. If I did, I probably wouldn't be writing this book (of course there is no "The Answer," as much as many self-help gurus would have you believe. Ever hear or read about some of their lives?). All I can say is, do something. Anything. Try a little harder. Because, while you may think your relationship is merely making a non-eventful pit stop...

Hey, can you tell the earth is moving right now? No? Exactly my point.

Ok, then. Get on it. And do it now. Not tomorrow. Not "soon." Not "when I get a chance." The clock is ticking. Now.

THE STATUS QUO

Remember, if you think your relationship is not going anywhere right now, you're wrong. It is. Look behind you. Glance up at the Relationship Rearview Mirror. There it goes...

FOR WANT OF A KISS GOOD-BYE

If I could tell thee I love thee
Yet one more time,
I would tell thee, not with sounds uttered,
Nay, lest they lead me anew to errors past.
Dare, I would profess to thee with
Ocean swells against thy soles,
The sand beneath thine feet and
My sweet touch against thy palm;
Words without lips, yet screaming from my heart.
For I would tell thee I love thee
From Life's unsilent Breath
With but another echoless chorus...
Of heeding ear and hushed lips
For thine wonted toils of prevalence,
Though not from mine's look of commonplace
But rapt listening of mine soul;
Hearken to as much of thine unsaid
As I have spoken with nonstated.
With these and each unsounded vow
I would tell thee I love thee,
So that my wisened silence now cried out louder
Than the labored words of whispered past.

Eric Champnella

OLIVE JUICE

GETTING OVER IT ALL

What does "getting over it" mean?

I ask this question because there are some days when it just doesn't feel like I'll ever know the answer to that question. Days when my memory is a curse. Days that the phrase "remember when..." seems profane.

You see, I once foolishly believed that "getting over it" meant waking up one day with little or no recognition, little or no memory, of this person who had caused me such happiness at one point, but now such great pain. Apparently I mistakenly believed that "getting over it" was from the lovelorn thesaurus, its synonym being "amnesia."

But, as with so many insights I gained for these pages, a friend of mine had a different view. My friend Todd, who went through a similar experience (what a shock), told me that you never do "get over" the person. Rather, he said, you learn to accept that you don't "get over" that person, learn to live with that realization and go forward that way.

And now, looking back through the unwanted perspective of "been there, done that," I am beginning to think his words just might be true. Which, contrary to how his theory may sound at first utterance, I believe may not be so bad after all.

To be honest, when he first told me his idea, I thought he was advocating a tormented future of regret and tainted memories. But that really isn't the case. I think he was merely stating the obvious - that it's impossible to erase the recollections and feelings of what was once love, no matter how terrible the end of that love now seems.

Maybe "getting over it" isn't the phrase we should even use because it's more a "moving forward." Letting go of the past, not by forgetting, but realizing that we will always remember. Always. Oh sure, the pain won't be as great. It might not even register as "pain" at a certain point. But "it" will be there. The scars of lost love.

Once we stop "trying to forget" and just accept that there is no memory erase button - no feelings voided switch - then I think we are on our way toward the healing process. Because even if we were capable of pressing that nonexistent button, its effects would only be temporary. Because a chance song on the radio, a scent in the air, a friend not seen in years is all it takes to break through the walls of "trying to forget" and bring the past rushing forward to the present. So there is no use trying to forget the past only to have it suddenly brought forth through no choice of our own. I guess we have to deal with it and not try to just push the pain and the memories all aside. They're not going anywhere. So why fight it?

Easier said than done, I know. Believe me. There are times when that "realization" is nothing more than a dull throb in the pit of my stomach. But you gotta just keep pushing on. And trust those who've traveled the same road.

As I learn to understand and accept that I will never "get over it" in the former meaning of those words to me, it somehow makes things and the future seem just a little easier. Even if the initial realization of that seems kind of tough to handle. Such is the result of personal insight at times.

It's funny because, as I debate back and forth as to the validity of the very words I've just written, every now and then, a well-meaning friend will say something to the effect of, "Don't worry, some day you're gonna meet someone who's gonna make you forget all about her."

But as I think of that now, as well-intentioned as those words are, I must say that I hope that doesn't happen. For, having become at least somewhat enlightened by the education of pain, I don't want to meet someone to help me to forget. Nope. The person I'm looking for is someone who will make it all right to remember.

OLIVE JUICE

The Poet's Rose

Neither Venus gaze on moonlit trail
Nor sunset's crest from ocean shore
brings me to these words.
Not warm embrace near fire's hearth
Or lips' caress on summer stroll
tempts me with true verse.
Nay,
Tis earthen gaze on moonlit trail
And fallen crest from ocean shore
that taunts me with repair.
From lone embrace near fire's hearth,
Days past caress on summer stroll
do poet's thoughts compare.
For my muse hides not
In rose-shed petals
But from her thorny side
As my quill fairs not
In clouded burst
Instead from tears collide.

Eric Champnella

OLIVE JUICE

SEARCHING FOR ANSWERS

At some point, you must stop looking for "The Answer." The one letter, phone call or face-to-face meeting that will wrap up all the loose ends and leave all questions, asked and unasked, resolved. Because there is no paragraph in the letter, no words on the phone, no glance at the lunch that will put all to rest and leave you feeling with a sense of finality. As I've stated before, that can only come from within.

I know it's hard to accept. It is indeed the most bitter of all pills to swallow. But it must be done. From my experience, and having talked to others, it seems we all think that if we could just "get all the answers" we could close up the remaining emotional loose ends from the damage done and move on. Just one more talk/chat/discussion on the matter. Please...

Don't be fooled.

It's not answers we seek, but a reprieve. A reprieve from the pain we are going through and will continue to go through until we come to terms on our own with what happened. For neither 100 letters, countless hours on the phone, nor a week's worth of lunches will provide the needed solace. There will always be one more doubt. One final query. One last request at explanation. That's because, just as love has no all encompassing definition for its best and most magic of moments, so too are there no adequate answers and or words to satisfy when love - or, more appropriately, its loss - is at its most painful.

There are no words of comfort from outside for the wounds of a broken heart within.

I feel quite the hypocrite as I write these thoughts down because I too sometimes get that gnawing need for one last emotional summit. When all things felt will be answered to satisfaction and I can just "move on" never to look back. All as a result of this final, comprehensive, Q&A session.

Yet, while I still occasionally feel this urge, I know it would not solve anything. Would not close all wounds. Rather it would merely cause pain with still more questions to those other answers. For what response is ever sufficient to the question, "Why did you break my heart?"

You know, I sometimes wish love was like a job. When a person leaves a job or is let go, often there is an "Exit Questionnaire" used to tie up loose ends and get answers so things can be improved in the future. Both parties can part ways having gotten and given the information they needed to make a clean break and move on.

Hmm. Might not be such a bad idea for relationships:

"Uh, Fred, I've met this really neat guy named Chuck and I'm going to move in with him. Therefore, I'd like to put in my two weeks notice."

"Ok, Kathy. I just need you to fill this out. Please answer questions one through...1,500 as completely as possible. And you can use the back if you need more space for your answers."

"All right. Thank you."

"No, thank you. Make sure you leave that on the kitchen table with the apartment key before you go."

And then they shake hands and part ways. Much easier, I think.

Barring the implementation of the questionnaire method, I guess we each just have to tough it out. Try to look forward as much as possible in the most painful moments when all we want to do is look back and ask, "Why?"

The Answers will come soon enough. In time. But not from the letters, calls or meetings with the former lover or spouse. No, the final answer to that "why?" will come from the touch of a previously unknown hand during a beachside stroll at sunset. From the laugh at a joke on a breezy fall afternoon. From the racing heart of a kiss on rainy spring day.

Then, without words or replies to questions asked, you will truly have The Answer.

OLIVE JUICE

THE INCONVENIENT

Love is about the inconvenient.

We often hear that "love is difficult." But I'd like to take that one step further. I think love is downright inconvenient.

As the cliché goes, "If it was easy, we'd all have it." Needless to say, we certainly all don't. And when we do finally "have it," often it's not for any great length of time. Because love is so...inconvenient.

Anybody or anything can last or be there when it is easy. But that is not love. Might seem like love. Might even feel like love in some instances. But it ain't the real McCoy. Probably closer to The Great Imposter - Infatuation. Infatuation is convenient. Infatuation is easy. But infatuation doesn't last because life itself is not easy. And of course, life is inconvenient. Infatuation gets tripped up in the complexities of life. Therefore, it must either grow and change into love or it simply falls by the wayside and perishes.

Hell, even writing about love is inconvenient. Trying to sum up something best described as magical is inconvenient. What words are there that haven't already been used? What sentences not already constructed? What thoughts does one utilize to adequately convey emotions that poets have only scratched the surface of?

Inconvenient. I guess that's why, besides being the most powerful thought expressed in the English language, love is also a four letter word. Ah, love.

But that's why love is indeed so special. For think of the most incredible things that have ever happened in your life. The things attained that you are most proud of. Chances are they came at great sacrifice and were not easy to get. But oh, the rewards. And isn't love the greatest reward of all?

Even though all this may seem like common sense, it's amazing how many people somehow "forget" or overlook the obvious when involved in a relationship. I know I did. I naively thought that once I was "in love," the easy part started. You could just kind of ride it out in all its glory. Well, I was wrong. You must do the work of love. The valleys are so deep only because the rewards of the mountaintop are so high. So great.

I think a big problem we have, myself included, is that when things aren't going well, we say that things aren't "right." But what we really mean is - things aren't perfect. Somehow we got the notion that love is supposed to be perfect. Too many movies. Too many romance novels. Too many happily ever after fairy tales.

Yet love isn't about movies, novels or fairy tales. Love isn't about perfect. Love is down and dirty. Love is hard. Love is about real life. And only when we come to the realization that things aren't perfect, only then can true love become "perfect" in its own way. I know that sounds like a quite a mess but I actually think it makes sense. You see, I kept waiting for the fairy tale myself, and that waiting for something that isn't real ruined the imperfectly perfect real-life fairy tale that I was living but didn't even realize.

Huh!?!?

I guess trying to explain all this is best described as downright inconvenient.

OLIVE JUICE

THE LAST KISS

I still remember...

An early May morning. One of those overcast days when it looks as though the skies might open up any minute with a mid-spring downpour - or simply continue on with the cloudy status quo.

On the way to the airport, the typical oh-my-God-did-you-forget-something rush out of her apartment was behind us as we settled in for the short ride to the Delta terminal. We both talked about how much fun this trip had been and yet how short it was. How short all trips are in a relationship when both parties know they will end with this same car ride every time and the bittersweet words, "See you soon."

We pulled up to the "Departures" curb at the airport. I grabbed my bags out of the back and sat in the passenger seat for a long moment finally broken by...

"See you soon."

"Very soon."

THE LAST KISS

Ah, those familiar words again. Followed by that uncomfortable silence. Which it seems there always is. Like there should be more profound words when two lovers part, no matter how brief the time away is supposed to be. Trying, wanting to say so much more and yet...

"Yeah, very soon."

And then I leaned over to her and we kissed good-bye. Nothing extra special. No postcard quality embrace fit for framing. No additional meaning hidden in the gesture. Just good-bye. And, of course, I love you. All summed up in one gentle moment.

And that was it. Our last kiss.

At the time, as I stood there on the curb, bags in hand, in front of those electronically controlled airport doors and watched her green Saturn pull off into the day, I had no way of knowing the significance of what had just happened. No way of knowing that maybe I should've tried to find better words. That "soon" now had no date. That we had just had our final embrace. I simply turned, and with the "whoosh" of the doors, headed for my flight.

I had no idea.

It wasn't like that when Humphrey Bogart kissed Ingrid Bergman good-bye at the end of "Casablanca." He knew that was to be their last kiss. Their final farewell. With her plane set to fly off into the night and with Claude Rains' "beautiful friendship" nearby to soften the blow, Bogie and all of us who've seen the movie, knew.

That's the trouble with life. There is no script and musical cue to point the important things out. There are no special moment Post-It notes. No Twilight Zone-esque monologues that alert us to the fact that our lives are about to change forever. Nope. We only become aware of these personal history altering events when we get a chance to recover and examine the little black boxes of our lives long after the mid-air explosion of Us flight #1313.

And examine we will. For in the aftermath of such a personal tragedy, while the heart may be shattered and the spirit may be pretty much in shambles, the little black box that is our memory will survive for later scrutiny. Showing us clues of impending disaster. A malfunction here. A stress fracture there. A faint warning light off to the side. And only then will the causes become clear, if they ever really do. Oh sure, "the experts" will say that no one was at fault. They'll rule out pilot error. They'll say that there was no way you could've seen it coming. No way to tell that the end was near. But still...

I guess we can never prepare for the unknown. The unexpected. The "not in a million years." For when one's in love and all appears well, nothing ever seems like it could be "the last time." There never should be a final hug in happily ever after. But, unfortunately there is. And sad to say, often we never even will know it at the time.

So while it may sound like a cliché or just plain common sense (and most clichés are just that), since we can never know a lot of the time when the end is drawing near for something beautiful (but even if we could somehow gaze into the crystal ball of life, that shouldn't change what I'm about to say), think of every moment together as the end. Treat every second like the last one. Greet every "I love you" like its final utterance. Taste every kiss like it was in truth, "Good-bye."

And while that won't soothe the pain of the end of "forever" if it does happen, at least when we do look back someday and study life's internal flight recorder, in our heart of hearts, we will each know that we truly realized what we had was love and cherished it accordingly. We'll know that we treated every second together like the unrepeatable time that it is. Enjoyed every day with one another to the fullest.

And you know what? Maybe if every day, if each second together, is truly lived like that, maybe, just maybe, there won't need to be an examination of that damn black box to search for clues. Because maybe there won't be a broken hearted good-bye.

But even if there is and even if Claude Rains isn't there to walk off into the night with us, at least we'll have lived each moment like it was the last kiss.

MAGIC MOMENTS

I have always considered myself a hopeless romantic. As far as I was concerned, in any good movie, boy and girl always wound up together by the time the credits rolled. Any other way would be, well, unromantic. Actually, to me, any other way would be downright wrong. A flat out sin. And, most likely, a waste of six or seven bucks.

But, I have to admit, sometimes being a hopeless romantic is bad. Bad in the sense that I think the "hopeless romantic" is quite often looking for that perfect movie-ending love. Trying to stay in that initial bliss/infatuation stage that never lasts. To put it bluntly, sometimes just plain "hopeless" - minus the romantic part. Because like M. Scott Peck said in his book, *The Road Less Traveled,* "It's after one falls out of love that true loving can start."

And I agree. Ninety nine point nine percent.

For on the other hand, while I obviously second the notion that one can't stay forever in the bliss stage, I do feel that one needs to be able to recapture it on occasion. To touch the reasons all over again. To fall in love once more with that special person. To find bliss now and then. Anywhere. Maybe on a long vacation or even just for a few brief moments on a walk through the park.

And when I say that, I'm not talking about on the walk simply thinking, "Geez, now I remember why I fell in love with her." No, I'm talking about actually feeling it again. Being taken back to the ol' pang-in-the-heart days even if for a moment. And in that moment, to recapture the actual feeling itself and not merely its fleeted memory. To not just recall, but to reawaken. To rekindle. To relive. Like the 50 year old alum who gets goosebumps when he walks across the campus for the first time in 30 years, we all need that magic moment now and then.

Everyone knows people who, by all accounts, are in love with one another but say, "The passion has died" or "the magic has faded." Yet they continue on in these "normal, healthy" relationships. However for those relationships to thrive and grow, to not simply fade away, to not stay on that same plateau, those truly magic moments must take place from time to time. Must because love is such hard work and sometimes it's difficult to see just how worth it that work is.

Now, to be honest, I have no idea if those things or "moments" (which make the events sound much too brief) are created through the above-mentioned hard work or if, in addition to it, they are something else. The unknown when two people just click. Just "know." (Don't we all kind of envy the people who say, "We just knew"? Knew what?! How?! I mean, I knew I loved my old girlfriend. I knew I could marry her. But yet, I didn't "just know.")

And don't be misled. I'm not talking about movie-type "just knows." Where some cheesy, halo-like special effect clues in the clueless in the audience. I'm talking about your friends, neighbors and co-workers. Those rare yet existing people we all hear it about from time to time. Those "just knowing" couples who give us all hope in the magic of love.

Are situations like that fate? Perhaps. And do you have to be "ready" to "just know" or does "just know" just happen?

Ah, the unexplained mysteries of Life and Love.

What? Are you sitting there reading this waiting for me to give you the answer? Ha. I haven't got the foggiest on this one. I was kind of hoping you had some answers here.

As a matter of fact, if you do, drop me a line. I'd love to hear others' thoughts on this ultimate puzzle, love's Gordian knot.

OLIVE JUICE

WHEN YEARS TURN INTO DAYS

As I flew back to California January 2 after spending the holidays with my family in Michigan, I figured I'd use the flight to do some thinking about a few resolutions for the just-started New Year. I knew I was supposed to do it prior to the big bashes of December 31st, but I guess I had procrastinated a tad too much during the now-passed holiday season. I guess there were just too many college football games with "national championship implications" I needed to watch to spend too much time needlessly thinking about "unimportant" stuff like how to better myself.

And as I tried to come up with some resolutions that I would keep at least until the end of the month let alone as life-altering changes in my day-to-day routine, I got to thinking about how interesting it is that we all divide our lives into chapters based on New Year's Day. How that is the turning point. I started thinking about how many times during the week leading up to New Year's Day I had heard some poor sap (myself included and just as guilty of the following charges) say, "Boy, I can't wait until the New Year." I both heard it and said it a lot. Too much on both counts.

But I got to wondering: Why must we wait until a champagne toast on New Year's Eve or a chat around a Christmas tree to look forward and change the negatives in our lives today? Whatever happened to the here and now? Maybe that's a fault with Western society in general - "Years." The measurement of years seems to be the dominant method of keeping track of the passage of time: He's 29 years old. I'll be a junior this year. We've been married 12 years. Etc., etc., etc. Maybe if we viewed each day as a bigger event, gave each day more seniority and importance, more value, maybe our lives over the (gulp!) "years" would be better. Maybe we should change the name of the passage of 24 hours to one "year" instead of one "day." Maybe we'd cherish each one of those new 24 hour "years" much more. Maybe we'd look forward to each as a lifetime of its own. Instead, we seem to wait until a great sickness befalls us or we reach old age before we realize the wonder, the joy, the miracle, of each and every day. When we only have a very short time left, only then do we appear to notice today. To savor the moment. While the rest of our lives we seem to look back but once at the end of every December to take stock of the preceding year; using that one day, January 1st, to make all the plans for the following.

I guess maybe it's just easier to keep track of things and events that way...but it sure would be easier to live, I think, by the other. The 24 hour "year."

OLIVE JUICE

AND STILL MORE LITTLE TIDBITS FROM THE JOURNAL

Moving On

Moving on is a dirt road. Looking back is an expressway.

I have come to this epiphanal conclusion as I examined my own healing process over the last couple of months. Anybody who has been through such pain knows it is so much easier to sit around one's apartment with the shades drawn watching redundant talk shows on the tube as you think about "the good ol' days." It's much more difficult to try to put it all in perspective from the outset and move forward.

Since I know there is no hope of reconciliation, that at least forces me to stare down the dirt road in my horse and buggy...even while the sports car and the on-ramp stand nearby. Always waiting.

Hmm.

"Giddy-up."

In Your Best Interest

You know, I think friends, family, ministers, counselors, etc. have to tell you that what happened is for the best and whatever you did in the relationship, even though it might have led to its downfall, is ok. Because, what if we didn't do it that way? I guess it's to keep us all, when faced with one of these situations, from speeding down that expressway day after day. Until we finally crash and burn on Lookback Highway.

These pages contain both the depressing and the hopeful. I trust one understands the importance of examining the former if any true, successful attempt is to made on the latter.

Shakespeare Would've Called

I'm beginning to think that "hopeless romantic" isn't a positive, cute, optimistic thing but rather a pathetic, unrealistic and clouded view of situational reality.

I sure wish I could be one of those guys who didn't care. One of those guys who, when someone screwed them over, they simply moved on with nary a glance back. Someone who didn't want to call. Someone who... Wait. Am I describing someone I really want to be? Am I describing someone who doesn't "care" in a good way or someone who doesn't feel? Would that new person I describe still feel as I do?

Hmmm.

Sure, while it's true that I think it is those very feelings that seem to do me in at times, these are also the feelings that allow me to keep this journal - with such openness and insight inside. Yet there has got to be a balance.

Believe me, even Shakespeare glanced backwards. And given the technology, he would've called!

To close yourself off from the potentially bad and painful is to also cheat yourself out of the absolute joy from the good. Life is not supposed to be an unsalted cracker, it is a gourmet feast - and should be lived accordingly.

But also, isn't there a way to lesson the impact of the bad and increase the ratio of the good parts? Instead of 1:1, can't we somehow make it, say, 4:1 odds - good over bad? Maybe that is the very key to life. Because I certainly don't need one painful experience to enjoy each joyful one. I believe too many people think they need to suffer in amounts equal to each "good" thing that happens in their life. When poet Kahlil Gibran says that joy and sorrow are but two sides of the same coin, how do we somehow weight the desired side to better our chances on each flip? If only I knew the answer...

Is there an answer? Here's a paradox, maybe the search is the answer (or the path). Or, maybe to stop continually searching and searching is the answer. Hmm. Just a thought.

On Falling In, Falling Out and Healing

Wow. Letting go.

Falling out of love is a much different process than getting into it. There are no skipped heartbeats. No great preludes. No fanfare. Nope, nothing like the magic of falling in love. Just a dawning realization. That's it. Nothing poetic. Certainly not pretty. Nothing even exciting. That's probably why poets write about falling in love, being in love and the heartache of broken/failed love (and don't confuse the last as "falling out of love" for it is quite the contrary. It is because one is still in love that the heartache hurts so very much).

TO AVOID OR NOT TO AVOID

I got to thinking today. (Uh-oh). I was thinking about what I wrote at the beginning of this book. About how I hope that maybe through this book, these words, I could somehow help someone avoid the pain I went through. Well, as I sit here and reflect, I don't think I could help anyone actually avoid the pain. Second of all, and more importantly, maybe that wouldn't even be best. Maybe the pain, to some extent, isn't so bad after all (trust me, I only have gained this theory/insight in hindsight. Not during. Believe me, during the fact, I think I would've enjoyed a hot poker in the eye more.)

You see, as I sit here in my way-too-hot-apartment, I think, just maybe, the pain I went through has actually served some sort of purpose. That it has been cathartic to some extent. Cleansing. I don't know. I feel much different. Better off in so many ways.

Oh no! Am I becoming one of "them?" The legions of friends and family who said just such a thing to me what seems like so many months ago, only to get my patented "Are you out of your &^%$*@ skull?" look when they proposed such lunacy? It looks that way.

Life is definitely better than any book I've ever read. More joy and pain. More twists and turns. More unique characters than one ever and never expected to appear.

All part of the story called life.

Only this story doesn't have a clear-cut beginning, middle and end. No three act structure. No predictable outcome.

It's more of an endless sequel.

I guess life was never meant to be easy. Never meant to follow any set route. Never meant to be "avoided."

So maybe I'm not supposed to help anyone circumvent these pains because 1) I can't and 2) maybe, just maybe, it's not for the best.

Now I understand that if you are currently in the "rock bottom" stage of heartbreak, despair or loss, this may seem like the biggest crock of self-help, writer b.s. you've ever heard. And I can't say you are wrong from where you probably currently sit (which is somewhere close to the emotional ledge. The heart abyss).

So why then do I continue to write these words and why do you continue to read if the pain is inevitable? Because, while it is indeed inevitable as you now probably know and feel all too well, you may not know that it is also indeed survivable. There is an o.k. tomorrow out there somewhere. An all right. An over the hump.

All part of the story of life.

The hardest part is the right now.

So maybe I'm not supposed to tell you how to avoid it, because that is impossible and not for the best, but rather I'm supposed to let you know that it can and will be all right. Will be better. Will be bearable.

So hopefully as that radio drones on with what was once "your song," while the picture on the shelf that was once a joyful wake-up sight is now only a cruel reminder, while the old greeting cards are set aside and stored in a little shoebox in the back of the closet, you'll at least know there is an o.k. out there somewhere down the road.

Take it from someone who fortunately or unfortunately speaks from experience. Someone who has at one time not so far away, felt just like you.

It's not avoidable only survivable.

OLIVE JUICE

FOREVER

I don't believe in forever anymore. I'm no longer a proponent of "happily ever after." I can do without "always."

Those are great words and ideas. Trouble is, they work best in fiction, songs and movies.

Now before you think I've turned in my Romantic's Dictionary for good, I haven't. Rather, I've replaced those words and ideas with better words and ideas. Words and ideas like "today." "Right now." "This moment."

Lately I've been thinking that too many of the supposed words of affection and love connote the tomorrow. The going to. The soon-to-be. Which is fine and dandy but I think a lot of times it comes at the expense of the here and now. And I now believe that it is a mistake. For I have come to the realization and conclusion that love is not about the abstract of tomorrow, but rather can only be fully realized in the concrete of today. For love is not a theory like "down the road," "Soon," or "someday." Love is about here. Love can only be felt and lived now. In this instant. The present.

Romance novels and movies tell us about "happily ever after" but never show it; the book or film always ending with the "happily ever after" part just around the corner. That's because real love reveals itself in the pain and problems of day to day. The complexities of "what next?"

I don't believe in forever anymore only because I have seen the error of my ways in waiting for the tomorrow only to be cheated of the today. For in fantasy, "happily ever after" starts at the end. In real life, it has already started.

IN SEARCH OF...

Once again, I turn to advice I received from my friends in order to pass along this next little chunk o' info to you:

My friend Kelli is one of the sweetest women I know. She has an incredible wit and a super sense of humor. Both became evident to me when she was telling me about The List or, as she called it, Searching for Mr. Right. Here's the story...

Kelli told me that she read or heard somewhere that in order to find your perfect mate, you must know exactly what you are looking for. Makes sense. How can you know if you don't really know? Still make sense? Anyway, she said a common theory (uh oh, sounds like *Cosmo* to me) is that one should compile a list of the 25 most essential qualities you seek in a mate as well as the 10 things you absolutely cannot tolerate. She claims that if the list is honest and accurate, you should find that person described in your list within a few short months. Like she said, "You can't effectively shop until you have written up your shopping list."

Well, here goes. I guess I'll give Kelli's list method a try. But if you see "1 box Cheerios" and "1 gal. Milk" anywhere on the list, please note that I've screwed up and confused this little exercise with a totally different list.

Hmm. Maybe that was my mistake in the first place...

SEARCHING FOR MISS RIGHT

1. Intelligent/Educated. (Doesn't need to be in Mensa but should at least know it's not a town in Arizona. Can name at least one former president who isn't on some form of currency. Prefers Jeopardy! over Wheel of Fortune.)

2. Athletic. (Former tri-athlete not a pre-req but likes to stay in shape. Has played two different sports, if only for fun, in the last year - not counting lawn darts or billiards. Would be one of the first to join in a volleyball game with friends at the beach even if she had never played before. This category also includes the enjoyment of watching at least one sporting event.)

3. Loving/Caring/Sensitive. (Actually gives a hoot about her fellow human beings. Able to give and receive love. At least got choked up at the end of "Ghost.")

4. Sense of Humor/Funny. (Doesn't need to laugh at all my jokes but at least knows I told one.

Has a ready smile. Realizes comedians on unicycles doing Jack Nicholson impressions or who say, "Here's a joke you can take home with you…" are not funny.)

5. Challenging. (Always pushing me and us to be our best both individually and together. Keeps me on my toes in terms of how I think and what I believe.)

6. Family Oriented. (Wants to raise a family even if it means we'd have to take one step back in our careers. Close with her siblings, parents, grandparents and any relatives not currently serving time. Also gets along with my family and doesn't consider seeing them something akin to jury duty.)

7. Mature with just a hint of the child still inside. (Responsible yet able to still see life with the wonder that we all once saw it with before we became "responsible." Wouldn't wear a halter top to church but might run through the sprinkler with the neighborhood kids. Correction: Would NEVER wear a halter top.)

8. Passionate (About life and love. Has convictions, but not of the courtroom variety. Able to give something her all because she believes in it.)

9. Goal Oriented. (Has things she wants to accomplish in life that are not related to shopping. However, she is not consumed by these things.)

10. Honest. (The only games she plays with me are of the board sort. Doesn't pretend the call in the middle of the night is her first grade gym

teacher when it is really her old boyfriend...again. And if things should ever not work out, would tell me face to face instead of with some disappearing act or a phone call.)

11. Forgiving. (Doesn't keep bringing up the fact that I once had to cancel a lunch date with her 7 years ago. Realizes that we all make mistakes - even if one of them was buying a WHAM! CD back in college.)

12. Spontaneous. (Everything we do doesn't have to be set up weeks in advance in her Day Planner. Would occasionally actually buy one of those flowers from the guy beside the freeway ramp - but not the bananas. Lives life to the fullest with the opportunities presented at the moment, not just those planned in advance.)

13. Doesn't take herself too seriously. (Even if she were to be the most successful businesswoman in the world, would still jump right into the previously-mentioned volleyball game even if she did look silly. Isn't afraid to try even if she makes mistakes. Would still admit that she once thought "Land of the Lost" was the greatest show on TV.)

14. Open minded. (Would understand when I mention that I once had a crush on half the cast from the Facts of Life. Accepts people for who they are. Willing to listen to a point of view that isn't hers.)

15. Goes for her dreams. (Still has a passion to achieve something that she always wanted to. Hasn't given up on those dreams because the

work-a-day world has stolen them from her. Doesn't merely accept what life has dealt out today, but tries to go for things to make a better tomorrow for herself.)

16. Shares her feelings. (Doesn't put me on the proverbial sh*t list simply because I forgot my mind reading pills for the day. Tells me what she's thinking and doesn't answer, "Oh nothing," when I ask. Let's me know what's inside even if it does make her vulnerable.)

17. My best friend. (We are a team. Still two separate individuals but I can tell her anything and not fear that it will come back to haunt me down the road. Simply put, we just fit. Makes it all worthwhile.)

18. Likes my family/friends. (Doesn't have to want to be adopted, but takes a genuine interest in my family. Will not cringe when my buddy tells her about "the ol' wild days" for the tenth time.)

19. Cute. (Let's face it, we have to be physically attracted to one another. My "type"? Hmm...Brown hair, nice figure, great smile and pretty eyes. The proverbial "girl next door" type.)

20. Affectionate. (Likes to hold hands. Doesn't need to be a PDA monster, but a kiss on the cheek for no apparent reason while we're out and about is a-o.k.)

21. Independent. (We're a couple, not two people joined at the hip. Still has her own beliefs, goals, dreams. Will vote for a different presidential candidate than me even if I think she's crazy. Not

beholden to her career, friends or even me.)
22. Outgoing/Friendly. (Treats people the way a first-day-on-the-job McDonald's counter employee would treat you. Fun to be around. Likes to talk. Isn't a bump on a log.)
23. Trustworthy. (I can tell her anything without having to preface it with, "Now don't tell anybody this..." Feels that secrets of the heart are just that.)
24. Happy. (Generally enjoys life. Can make even an overcast day o.k.)
25. Interested in me. (Personally, sexually, etc. Does not give her own identity up but likes me for who I am inside, not what I "do." Actually means it when she says, "How was your day?")
26. Similar tastes...to an extent. (I can still say tomato and she can say tamoto but generally at least agree on the major issues in life. Yet, when we don't, she will challenge my way of thinking.)
27. Understanding. (Even if she doesn't like college football, understands why I feel the need to watch the highlights six times a Saturday during the fall on ESPN. Is there in the bad times as well as the good because she understands that's how life, love and relationships are sometimes.)

Yes, I know that was more than 25, but one just can't leave anything out when looking for The One.

And now here's the flip side:

THE THINGS I CANNOT HAVE

1. Unfaithful. (Does not flirt with any of my relatives, friends and/or co-workers. Yes, staying up all night, naked in bed, drinking wine with your old boyfriend, even if you were "just talking" is still grounds for dismissal.)

2. Jealous. (Of my work, family or friends. Realizes that as important as she is in my life, there is still room for other things. Doesn't accuse me of hitting on the waitress because of the way I said "I'll have a large orange juice.")

3. Selfish. (Does this really need an explanation?)

4. Insecure. (Is sure of who she is. Emotionally stable. As my friend Kelli says, "Is not neurotic, psychotic or any other `otic.'")

5. Moody.

6. Money hungry/Materialistic. (There are going to be good times and bad but they will not all be dependent on our bank account. Secure in our love because of who we are as people not what other people see us as or what we have. Isn't bothered by the fact that I tell people I got my kitchen table at a garage sale like that's something to be proud of.)

7. Unmotivated. (Doesn't wait for life to come to her, but goes out and takes advantage of what life has to offer. Self-starter. Doesn't just sit around and...oh, never mind.)

8. Conditional love. (Loves me without the

words "when" or "if" attached. Doesn't make me feel that I'm always walking on egg shells in order to "earn" her love. Realizes there will be mistakes on both sides and love was never meant to be perfect. Doesn't use love as a weapon to be taken and given as needed to gain something.)

9. Petty/spiteful. (Is big hearted, not mean or vengeful. Lets the small little things roll off her back. No grudges over something her lockermate said in sixth grade.)

10. Asexual. (Contrary to some schools of thought, sex between two people in love is an important part of a relationship. Obviously it's not number 1 [but top 3 is cool!], yet it should actually be something looked forward to by both parties - and not just on the honeymoon.)

11. Judgmental. (Waits for the facts. Isn't quick to point the finger. Will actually admit mistakes if they were hers and not simply try to "get out of it.")

Of course there had to be more than 10 of these ones, too!

Well, there they are. The outline for The One. That was actually kind of fun to do. Try it sometimes. It's kind of neat to sit down and say, "This is really what I want." Does it work? We'll, or at least I'll, find out.

In wrapping up this section, I'd like to quote Kelli again. She ended her own list with these words:

"Well, there it is...my key to happiness. The gateway to my glorious future. The key to finding the ultimate man who will sweep me off my feet and carry me off into the sunset. (Actually if he will just sweep the kitchen once in awhile and is able to carry me at all, I will be more than elated!)

I wrote down this list in the hopes that this `shopping list theory' that they have is true and that Mr. Right really is just around the corner. However, whether he is or is not waiting in the wings doesn't change the person I am. And contrary to the popular belief that you have to 'have somebody in your life' in order to be happy and to be a contributing member of society, I am basically happy and a pretty great person. But I imagine that this is because I do have someone in my life...ME!! And I am the best ME that I know how to be and my life is pretty complete and pretty great...So there!"

Couldn't have said it better.

OLIVE JUICE

TIME TO WIND THIS UP

Talking to a good friend one day recently, I asked her to listen to an entry I had just finished for this book. She said, "Oh what, still working on your `You broke my heart and left me for dead' book?"

Hmm.

Now, while she was joking, her comments gave me pause. I sincerely hope that's not what this book is. If it seems that way to you, the reader, I apologize. I have definitely missed the mark. However, her words did make me stop and think just where the end of this book should be. Whatever it is.

And as I sat here and realized that I'm almost coming up on the one year anniversary since I started this manuscript, I figured maybe it was time to think about wrapping it all up. Start to head for the home stretch. To bring this chapter of my life, the writing of this book, to a close. To find The End.

I look back to the time when I started this

thing and two things jump to mind. First of all, I can't believe I wrote and finished this. Wow! Who would've thought that I'd actually complete this little baby. The words in that journal were just my own personal way of helping myself through the most painful of moments. I never thought it would lead to this, whatever "this" has become.

Second, I'm smiling right now and actually a little sad. Smiling because I never thought when I first started jotting some of these words down in my journal that I'd ever get to the point where I could look back and smile at them. I hope that gives even the most shattered person reading these pages at least the hint of something better to come even if it seems so far away right now. And I'm a little sad because I'm actually going to miss putting these words to paper (or more appropriately, to keyboard) for this "journal." It's been fun. I kind of hate to let it all go. But like I said at this book's start, you never know when one part of your life is coming to an end and a totally different part is about to begin. So I think it's time for the "writing of this book" part to wind its way down...as a totally unknown chapter of my life is about to be "written." Explored. Lived.

I know many of the entries on these pages may appear very similar to one another and often they seem to be saying just about the same thing as something you read just pages before. I know. It's just that, sometimes I'd think of a little different way to say the words or make my point. Instead of feeling redundant, I hope each one was entertaining, worthwhile and enjoyable. It's so personal in places, I feel like I've actually had you, the reader, over to my house for the last couple of hours and we just finished sitting down and having a great chat over a cup of hot chocolate (I know coffee would've sounded better there but I don't drink the stuff).

Also, I sincerely hope somebody out there at school, home or work reading my little thoughts and such got something out of this. I know I did just putting these words down. And if you did, that would make it all worthwhile.

In fact, if you did "get something" out of this book, whatever that means to you, or even if you didn't, I'd love to hear from you. Write and tell me your thoughts, comments, etc.:

Eric Champnella
P.O. Box #132
11271 Ventura Blvd.
Studio City, CA 91604

Or, if you're feeling cyber, e-mail me at:

Eric@OliveJuiceBook.com

Well, I feel like I should have some insightful, poignant summary paragraph here. Like I should draw these pages to some meaningful conclusion. You know what? I can't.

Maybe that's it right there. A truism for life. After all the turmoil in life, can anyone truly, "sum it all up?" If anyone can, I've yet to see them do it in print anywhere.

I guess it can't be summed up. It just goes on. You know, that almost makes sense.

Life is tough. Difficult. Never easy. And yet we still must press on and consume as much of life, both good and bad, as we can. For if we do not, life will consume us.

I've learned that I'm going forward because to stay stagnant is not stagnant at all, it is to wither away. And I enjoy life too much for that.

And so I press on, "mindful of yesterday's demise" and still "waiting for the epiphany." Hmm. I think "waiting" might be the wrong word. Poetically it's right but waiting implies someone simply gives it to us. Yet the best things in life aren't given to us, rather we must seek them out and go after them with full force. Full vigor.

So I guess I should change that line of thinking and move forward from today - *searching* for the epiphany.

Thanks for reading. I'd like to finish this book and say good-bye with one of my favorite poems I wrote during this period.

OLIVE JUICE

Two Stars Falling

I sit here alone
And yet I can't help but wonder
Where you are right now.
What you are thinking,
Just what you are like.

I wonder how we will meet -
Chance encounter or Friendly nudge.
Will it be Love at first sight?
Knowing in an instant or
Must Time play His part.

Am I all you had hoped
Alone late at night?
Are you the strange face
In my wishes and dreams?

Has your Heart been tested
By other false meetings?
Or am I your first journey
Down Love's challenged path?

What will we do? What will we say?
Those first words
At Destiny's fated moment.
Suddenly afraid, for
maybe you

what if

how will

Then somehow I smile, just
Thinking of You.
Never seen. Never met.
And yet I know you.
So I sit here alone.

And I can't help but wonder...

Eric Champnella

OLIVE JUICE

If you would like to order additional copies of **Olive Juice,** please visit...

www.OliveJuiceBook.com